SHOW ME A NIGGER AND I'LL SHOW YOU A RACIST

The Mind Of A Psychopathic Genius

Yahdon Israel

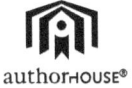

authorHOUSE®

AuthorHouse™
1663 Liberty Drive
Bloomington, IN 47403
www.authorhouse.com
Phone: 1-800-839-8640

First published by AuthorHouse 5/13/2009

ISBN: 978-1-4389-7661-7 (e)
ISBN: 978-1-4389-7659-4 (sc)
ISBN: 978-1-4389-7660-0 (hc)

Printed in the United States of America
Bloomington, Indiana

This book is printed on acid-free paper.

PREFACE

The lines on the cover represent the boundaries given by society to infringe individualism. Ironically, it is these same boundaries that determine the individual. Society gives us boundaries as individuals, but it is the individual who accepts them. No one can make you do what you don't want to do. We need conventional consensus to determine who we are as individuals. Without it we become followers of society, not knowing our own meaning of life. The mind of an artist cannot be contained forever, as the lines on the book change so does the boundaries of society. These sudden and radical changes are designed to imprison the minds of those who rebuke formal structure and etiquette. Keeping the control within the establishment, keeps the establishment controlled within itself. Because the establishment always changes itself, it always changes the individual. In due time these lines become nothing more than translucent enigmas used to show us our true colors. When we see that our individualism is cliché and trite, we no longer hold it to the same satisfaction. In order to preserve our "perfection" we stay within the boundaries we are given to remain individuals. This makes our perspective all the more real. Delusions of grandeur become the epic tale of our lives. As Olympians, we fight the establishment created by Titans to preserve our individualism. But when we get what we want, we cast ourselves to Tartarus because we cannot stand our true selves. To preserve godliness, humanity will conceal past faults and shortcomings for the "greater good." To preserve humanity, these same "gods" will reproduce. To be human means to be god, to be god means to be human. To accept it is godly, to deny it is human. Life is Satire.

"What really knocks me out is a book, when you're all done reading it, you wished the author that wrote it was a terrific friend of yours and you could call him up on the phone whenever you felt like it."

"Niggas Gonna Hate Me When They Finish *This* Book"

"People never believe you."

"Yes they will Holden."

"All morons hate it when you call them a moron."

"I'm not calling them morons."

"People never give your message to anybody."

"This message will be passed on."

"Don't ever tell anybody anything. If you do, you start missing everybody."

"I won't miss anybody, they'll miss me."

"I do believe he cared just as much for his people as white folks does for their'n."

"Thank You Huck, sometimes Holden doesn't get the point."

"I knowed he was white inside."

"But it's not about black or white it's about niggas."

"Well, if I ever struck anything like it, I'm a nigger. It was enough to make a body ashamed of the human race."

"Sometimes I do feel ashamed."

"I realized what a ridiculous lie my whole life has been."

"Mines too Biff, but I got to keep scratching the surface, no matter how tedious it may be."

"A small man can be just as exhausted as a great man."

"I'll take a vacation when I'm dead Ms. Loman."

"There was a time when I believed that too, Tom."

"Tell me about Miss Maudie, I grew up under both."

"Who asked you Holden? Wait! isn't you catholic?"

"I'm not Catholic; I'm just a regular nigga"

"That can be agreed upon Scout, good-lookin. And you know I gotta look out for females on this one right Mary? "

"I hold everybody to the same standard, so I know what you mean. I love niggas."

for the beloved. The lover alone possesses his gift of love. The loved one is shorn, neutralized, frozen in the glare of the lover's inward eye."

"Damn Ms. Morrison! You always sayin' something deep but I realized that to love people you have to distance yourself from civilized standards"

"Nature knows no indecencies; man invents them."

"That's what I thought Twain, but niggas be tellin me I'm wildin'."

"I reckon I got to light out for the Territory ahead of the rest, because Aunt Sally she's going to adopt me and sivilize me, and I can't stand it. I been there before."

"So have I Huck, you ain't never lie."

"Art is a lie that makes us realize the truth."

(This nigga Picasso still creating masterpieces) "If it aint art, its words, you a cool dude. But with all these lies it's hard to tell what's real and what isn't."

"If you tell the truth you don't have to remember anything"

"Well by the time this book is done Mr. Twain, nobody will remember anything, it'll be like the world never existed."

"Man is the measure of what exists."

"Wateva Protagoras, Sophists always complicating shit."

"The ego is not master in its own house."

"Damn Freud you fucked me up, just when you think you understand life, you never do, Mark take us to the book I'm done talking to these niggas. Oh and do it like you used to do."

"Persons attempting to find a motive in this narrative will be prosecuted; persons attempting to find a moral in it will be banished; persons attempting to find a plot in it will be shot."

"You ain't miss a beat my nigga, it's like you never left. You gotta do my eulogy!"

"James you made it! And just in time too, I'm about to do like my nigga Common did on Finding Forever."

"What?"

"Start the Show!"

"Show

"Y

The word "nigger" has been described as the most derogatory word in all of the English language. This word has become the self-fulfilling prophecy for every person of color that has died in vain trying to protect their dignity. With this word you can effectively trace the history of a people. This word, which was originally designed to destroy the psyche, ironically built the self-esteem of a nation. In recent times, there has been much debate as to who can use the word. White-Americans claim that racism is dead so it should be okay. African-Americans argue that to say that word, you have to be a part of the struggle. Experts say that the word should be stricken from the mouths of all that use it, whites, blacks and in-betweens alike. The NAACP went a step further by having a "funeral" for the word "nigger." All of these methods used to kill the word "nigger" and yet none have been successful. Many people still believe that "niggers" are alive and well. To believe that "niggers" are still walking amongst us insinuates that people still follow Americas' biggest illusion, the existence of the "nigger." If "niggers" do exist, point one out.

Illusion, the most dangerous concept that the human cognition can grasp, can effectively make peoples' ideals become reality. An illusion is a misrepresented image presented to the vision. An illusion deceives or misleads intellectually. Illusions cause people to misapprehend the actual nature of something, therefore making it false. An illusion is a set of patterns capable of reversing perspective. With illusion, nothing is as it seems. Illusion disrupts human cognition because it corrupts the brains' ability to correct itself. When this happens, the brain is unable to develop properly because it is set on an orbit that repeats itself. If the brain continues to repeat itself it will never actually correct the problems in which it faces. Instead, it will translate every problem into the one that is currently unsolved.

People don't usually accept things until they are seen. That is what makes an illusion so dangerous. Because an illusion is perceivable to the senses, it conflicts the perception of reality and fantasy. Ventriloquism, a major form of illusion, pleases the audience by making the impossible

possible. A ventriloquist holds a puppet and makes the puppet capable of moving its lips. Now that may seem acceptable, but when words appear to escape the puppets' mouth fascination occurs. You wouldn't normally be fooled by this event, but when you look at the ventriloquists' mouth you don't see him talk. That sets off a distortion in the brain, because now the impossible has just become possible. This leads to a fascination with fantasy because the fantasy now becomes perceivable to the senses.

It is a fact that dolls can't talk but you don't see the ventriloquists' mouth move, you only see the puppets'. Because you have physically experienced this, you now believe it's real. Usually, people will watch the ventriloquist to see if he ever moves his mouth. If there is never an occurrence where this action transpires then the audience will become even more enticed by illusion. However if there is a single flaw within the ventriloquists' show, the illusion is shattered and the show is no longer entertaining. When an illusion loses the power to unite reality and fantasy, it also loses the power to control and captivate.

An illusion has the ability to entrap one's perception, intelligence, and consciousness within the control of the illusion itself. In other words, an illusion can allow a person to believe that they're whatever the illusion dictates. However, if this illusion was to be shifted off of its axis, it could destroy the consciousness of a person leading them to confusion, displacement and insanity.

Like a house of mirrors, an illusion works the same way. Illusions, like a mirror, can reflect one image off itself and multiply it by an infinite number. Soon the illusion gives you different shapes, sizes and forms of the same concept. As you begin to see basic concepts take many forms, you become intrigued by it. Not questioning the legitimacy of this occurrence causes a fascination with the illusion. Before you know it, you are swept up in illusions' hurricane not knowing reality from fantasy. Illusion is twice as powerful as fantasy and reality. Although fantasy and reality are heavily dependent upon one another, they are separate concepts. You cannot define reality unless you can distinguish it from fantasy, and vice-versa. However, illusion intertwines reality and fantasy, making it one big concept, thus making it difficult to distinguish a difference. In order to understand the basis of an illusion, you must understand concepts that set up the foreground to what makes an illusion.

Reality is the quality or the state of being true. A reality is practical matters concerning authenticity. Reality, not being artificial or spurious, is a concept that exists regardless of being perceived or thought of. It is perceivable to the senses and can provide physical sensation as well as mental inspiration. A reality is no less than what is stated, and is worthy of a name. The name, whatever the case may be, gives the reality an existence that brings a concept into actuality. Reality changes perspective, perspective doesn't change reality. To explain my point further, Michael Jordan played for the Chicago Bulls. That is a reality that can be proven. No matter what a persons' perception tells them that doesn't change its actuality.

Fantasy, on the other hand, requires creative imagination and unstrained fancy. A fantasy is a capricious idea that reflects conceit and perspective. It is an imagined event or sequence of mental images usually fulfilling a wish or psychological need. A fantasy relies heavily on self-conception and individual thought. Fantasies show no flaws in individual perspective. A fantasy is an imperfect concept because it lacks the essential components necessary to make it reality. Perception can always change fantasy but can never change reality. Michael Jordan being a Bull is a fact, but the assertion that he's the greatest player in basketball is a fantasy. Michael Jordan's status reflects the perspective of the person. It can be proved that he is a Bull, but there is no ultimate definition for a "greatest player" so that assertion will remain individual thought.

A reality consists of everyone's fantasy. Reality is unbiased, so it has an equal limitation on everyone's fantasy. Reality at some point or another has crushed someone's ideas. Reality's impartiality evokes equality. Reality doesn't cater to any one person's idea. Because a reality heavily influences everyone's perspective, it can be accepted by anyone. Without a fantasy the human race will fill uninspired and unmotivated.

This will cause stagnation in the race causing the species to die off. The dividing line between fantasy and reality is that reality influences perspective whereas fantasy is influenced by reality. Direct cause and effect, Newton's third law of motion dictates this.

Newton's third law states that for every action, there is an equal and opposite reaction. For example, if you were to punch someone in the face, the action would be you punching them, and the reaction would be them getting punched. Now, that may be a fundamental scientific understanding, but it seems to escape the average cognition of human perception.

A vivid example of Newton's third law of motion and illusion is regularly seen in child rearing. We have all done something in our childhoods that has caused us to get punished. It is through trial and error that we mature our brains and develop our own perceptions. What's interesting about both concepts is that although they are all scientific ideas, they tend to often conflict with human nature. For example, you are playing one day in the house, and you break a lamp. According to Newton's third law of motion, the action would be you breaking the lamp, and the reaction would be the lamp breaking. That may seem simple, but this is when reality fantasy and illusion begin to conflict each other.

In reality, you broke the lamp and the lamp is broken, period. When your mother gets home, she asks you who broke the lamp, you tell her you did, and she chastises you for it. Most kids often ask what are they being punished for, and the answer is because they broke the lamp. These are all occurrences in reality, however, when the child is shown that these are the effects of breaking something, a distortion is perception happens. Fantasy has now become present in the child's mind. Because the child broke the lamp, the lamp broke. That is the action and equal and opposite reaction. The mother chastising the child and showing the child the "reaction" to a broken lamp causes the child's brain to neglect a basic reality. In addition, the child now asserts the perception that if something is put out then the same will be given back.

This intertwines reality and fantasy, making it an illusion. Whenever a fantasy is introduced within reality and the brain is unable to distinguish the difference that is called illusion interruption. So in response, the child's perception now adapts to its new presented situation, and believes that if good is put out then good is given back, and if bad is given then bad is received. This belief conflicts with Newton's third law of motion, because originally the child would see that the effect of its playfulness was a broken lamp. But the parents' chastisement now corrupts the original concept by reversing action and equal and opposite reaction to action equals same reaction.

The foreground of illusion is heavily present in human nature. The mind corrects itself by distinguishing reality from fantasy, but when illusion interruption is introduced it becomes more troublesome. To go further into the example, the child learns that if they break a lamp, they will be punished. So, because the child now knows that this is the reaction for a broken lamp. They begin to avoid lamps in efforts to preserve livelihood. The child has now deemed that being punished is unfavorable, so breaking lamps is bad. More noteworthy than that, the child's brain now believes that not breaking lamps doesn't receive punishment, making it favorable, and now asserts the knowledge that not breaking lamps is good. The more the child begins to figure out how the world works, the more confused the child becomes.

Now the child begins to set up situations where a favorable outcome can occur. For weeks following, the broken lamp is replaced with a new one. The child knows from past experience that they cannot break the lamp, or they will be punished, so they avoid it. Now, the child believes that they have done something good. They have not played near the lamp, so the lamp did not break. That is the original law of motion; however they have learned that favorable actions should be met with favorable reactions.

When the child's parent returns, the child tells the parent of their favorable action. In order to emphasize cause and effect, the parent may reward the child with a toy or treat. Again, the child's perception is distorted further. Its reality and fantasy is now one, this child is now living in an illusion. Because the child's mind can't distinguish between the two concepts, the child no longer bothers and begins to accept illusion as their reality.

Another occurrence transpires in which the child is faced with the lamp. The child, now seeing both favorable and unfavorable consequences, can now decide their fate. If the child wants a reward, they won't break the lamp. If a child wants chastisement, they will. Human nature dictates that the preservation of life is the primary concern of all living things, so the child will not choose an unfavorable fate; instead, they will go with the opposite. The parent returns, once again the child tells the parent that they have not broken the lamp. If the child doesn't receive a favorable reward, the child becomes confused and maybe even angry. This is the event that shifts illusion interruption off its axis. Whenever an event doesn't correlate with an illusion, it disrupts the brain. If the illusion cannot adapt to its peculiar situation quicker than the brains' ability to correct itself then the illusion is broken and reality is restored. This is called reality intervention.

The child was shown the effects of favorable and unfavorable causes. However the child did not receive a favorable reaction for their favorable action, so the child becomes withdrawn from the parent. That is the dangers of illusion; an illusion can combine many aspects as one. In this case, the illusion caused the child to believe that two separate events could be classified as one. Although the broken lamp ultimately caused the child to get punished, it is not the direct cause, but the inability of distinguishing reality from fantasy led the child's adoption of illusion.

Next there is the infamous war strategy, divide and conquer. To divide presents the ability to separate a whole into parts. Methods of division include classifying, categorizing, and differentiating. It is through division that we are able to conquer or control things. To conquer something entails that an opposition must be controlled by mental or moral power, it also includes gaining mastery by overcoming obstacles in opposition. When placing these concepts together you have the biggest tool for any illusion.

Divide and conquer is the oldest concept in war stratagem. Aside from it being the oldest, this is also the most dangerous tactic used in war. More dangerous than brute strength alone, divide and conquer allows the wielder to defeat the opponent without physical force. Divide and conquer relies heavily upon the mind. Whatever the mind does, the body will follow. So if you can successfully divide a persons' mind, you can successfully divide their body. Divide and conquer operates by finding differences within group, then using these differences to promote envy, distrust, hatred and violence within the body of the organization. With these four factors, the group begins to divide themselves using similarities and differences to categorize certain members within the group. As time transpires, the group becomes weaker in number due to the division of their own factions. Finally, the group is stripped down to its weakest state, which makes the group easier to conquer. This concept is applied in emotional intelligence.

Me
ah

Emotional intelligence regards the ability to monitor and understand one's own or other's emotions. Emotions are a mental state that arises spontaneously rather than through conscious effort. When you are emotional, you often act on impulse. Emotional people often disregard inhibitions that restrict them from free expression. When emotions are present, things are often done at whim and require little to no premeditated thought. Emotions often omit consequences and deals directly with present action. This may sound dangerous, but not if you can successfully divide and conquer them.

Understanding emotions is similar to understanding polarity. Emotions, like polarity, are defined by opposite extremes. They correlate the possession or manifestation of two opposing attributes, tendencies or principles. To define an emotion you need an extreme situation that causes a spontaneous reaction. This spontaneous reaction evokes emotion because there is no time for the brain to understand, organize, and consciously deal with the situation. For example, when you feel "good" your brain transmits messages to the brain that satisfies your perception. When this happens, your perception is amplified by reality and your brain now takes the given situation and classifies it as "good."

Your perception amplifies this feeling to the extreme to preserve its effect. The brain, being pushed to an extreme, now responds by producing the polarity of the initial feeling. Your perspective accommodates this change by classifying anything that is not desirable as "bad." Good is defined as anything that contributes to the original nature of something. Something that is deemed good has desirable effects meaning that the effects are highly sought to reproduce. In contrast bad is undesirable, disagreeable and disturbing. If something is categorized as "bad" then it conflicts with a person's perspective of what is desirable. This disturbs the mind and causes the person to avoid "bad" things in order to sustain life.

Now, that you can successfully understand what makes bad and what makes good, you can divide them. To do this requires categorizing familiar situations with ideal outcomes. If the outcome reflects a desirable thought then it satisfies the perspectives' end, making it good. However, if an outcome occurs that is undesirable it disturbs the reality and makes it bad. When these concepts have been divided they can then be controlled. Emotions can be controlled when they are understood. When someone understands their emotions, they are able to summon them at will. The exceptional ability to divide and conquer emotions allows a person to control their emotions. Those who cannot completely understand their emotions usually become unstable and fickle.

Actors would be the archetype for how to divide and conquer emotions. Actors have the task of portraying something that is not their actual nature. It is task that divides the good actors from the bad actors. Good actors study the role that's supposed to be portrayed and replicate it. Before they are able to do this, they must understand their own emotions. Emotions are the blueprint to someone's perspective. Emotions are like the DNA to personality. If an actor can understand their emotions and what triggers their emotions' response, they can now understand another person's.

A good actor studies a person, using emotional intelligence as their forefront, to understand what makes them unique. Once there is a basic understanding, the actor translates the person's problem into their own. If they can understand what triggers certain emotions then they can summon the emotion at will. When an actor can make someone else's emotions their own, that's when the task is complete.

When watching Russell Crowe in Gladiator, many people were captivated by the performance he was able to execute. In the year 2000, Russell Crowe was able to deliver a character that was uncanny to a soldier in the Roman Empire. So much so, this movie won five Academy Awards including Best Picture. Crowe, winning Best Actor, made the fantasy of a Roman general become a reality. In order for this performance to gain its power, Crowe had to study the life of an early

A.D. Roman. He learned the jargon of the Romans for that era. Crowe learned the morals of the Roman people. He studied the Roman Army and their battle tactics as well as the life of a slave. In due time, Russell Crowe became a Roman.

"When in Rome, do as the Romans do" that was Crowe's approach. When visiting a new place you should to accommodate the people of the mother country as much as possible. Watching this movie you would swear that Crowe was raised with Roman parents. His character was Maximus Decimus Meridius, a Hispano-Roman general who was betrayed by the emperors' son. Maximus, being favored by the emperor before his untimely death, is arrested and ordered to be executed at the hands of Commudus. Although Maximus escapes his demise, his wife and son are burned alive and crucified. Due to the shock of his wife and son's death, he faints and is picked up by a slave owner who holds Maximus in captivity.

While in captivity, Maximus assumes the new identity of "Spaniard." In the past he fought for honor, glory, pride, and dignity. As the "Spaniard." Maximus has to fight for the entertainment of others as a gladiator. His master takes notice to the exceptional talent he has as a fighter and tells Maximus that they will go to the Coliseum in Rome. Maximus, having revenge one his mind, is determined to do nothing else but avenge his family's death and the death of his mentor Marcus Aurelius. With one goal in perspective, Maximus is able to defy every law of Roman etiquette to be seen by the man who betrayed him. After Maximus changed a "fixed" battle, he was sought after by Emperor Commudus on his fantastic performance.

Commudus comes down to the arena and asks Maximus what his name is and asks him to remove his mask. Maximus defies the emperors' orders by turning his back towards the emperor. In Roman culture it was highly offensive to turn your back towards the emperor. The consequence for that was fatal, and could mean execution on site and Maximus knew this. He turns around and takes off his mask revealing his true identity, Maximus Decimus Meridius. Distraught and shocked Commudus orders that Maximus be executed. Ironically, it is Maximus' exceptional ability to fight which causes him to be spared at the hands of the people. Because it is Commudus ultimate desire to be loved by everyone and be remembered as the greatest emperor Rome has ever seen he is forced to allow Maximus to live.

Commudus, heavily conflicted with the reality of his past and the fantasy of his present, begins to create the ultimate illusion. He knows that he cannot have Maximus executed because that will disappoint the people. But he cannot allow Maximus to leave because that will live him vulnerable to exposure. He combines his fantasy of being loved by the people and his reality of being hated by Maximus and makes the ultimate illusion. Maximus is placed into situations where the odds are stacked against him to lose. The traps that are set up for Maximus' demise reflects Commudus' hostility, but in the eyes of the people it is all entertainment. Commudus has successfully merged his fantasy and his reality, welcome to illusion interruption.

Commudus now believes that he will triumph in this battle. He has used his worst nightmare and his greatest dream to produce the ultimate entertainment for the people. The problem arises when Commudus himself begins to be controlled by his own illusion. He felt that the combination of these concepts was the perfect plan. It pleased the people and it would make his intentional action of wanting Maximus dead look entertaining. What could go wrong?!?!

Maximus, using his only talent, slowly begins to destroy Commudus' illusion. Maximus was able to shatter every challenge given to him by Commudus. This began to show Commudus that the only one controlled by his illusion was him. Commudus was destroyed, but he would not leave without one more illusion. He decided to fight Maximus himself. This epic battle would pit him, the people's emperor, against Maximus, the people's champion. The winner of this battle will capture the hearts of the people and get the revenge that they always wanted.

Before the fight, Commudus visited Maximus in his cell. While talking to Maximus, he asks him for a warm embrace. During this embrace,

Maximus is stabbed in his chest and the wound is covered with armor. Maximus, with a stab wound in his chest, must now fight the person who has destroyed his illusion. Commudus is the man that killed his mentor, crucified his son, and raped his wife. Because Maximus' illusion was already destroyed, he had no problem destroying Commudus' illusion. Even with a stab wound, Commudus is still unable to kill Maximus. When Maximus is able to disarm Commudus of his sword, Commudus asks his men for a sword.

His soldiers, conflicted between illusion interruption and reality intervention, remain in a frozen psychological state where they no longer hold him to the authority that he was given. Because the title of emperor held so much power, it destroyed the soldier's illusion to see the person who they were taught to fear be defeated by a slave. Especially when they witnessed their emperor cheat. This confusion led to the breaking of illusion. In result, the soldiers began to think for themselves and decided not to help him. With Commudus' last illusion shattered by reality, Maximus is finally able to get his revenge by stabbing him in the throat.

After Commudus is killed, Maximus orders that the men of his battalion be freed. In addition, he orders that the power be given back to people. This command reflects the teachings of his mentor, Marcus Aurelius. Maximus, being reunited with his illusion, is able to die peacefully. He returns Rome to the people, and he is reunited with his wife and son…

For Russell Crowe to capture this role he had to understand his own fantasies and realities. Crowe had to study every emotion and understand them. In addition, he had to know what situations in his life triggered these emotions. When this was achieved he could now become his given character, Maximus Decimus Meridius. He understood that Maximus was a man of high stature that had his world crushed by the envy of a person he thought admired him. Crowe understood that Maximus had his mentor killed and wife and son murdered. Crowe sifted through all his emotions and matched the emotion with this given situation.

But Crowe is not actually Maximus, so how is this possible? Crowe's wife was not murdered, his mentor wasn't killed by someone, he wasn't a slave, and he's not Roman, so how could he capture the intensity of this character? What Crowe did was replace these "fantasies" with his "realities." Crowe began to apply the situation to his life. The specifics would come later but if he could understand a situation in which he was someone of high stature reduced to something lower by the jealousy of a supposed friend he could understand the psyche of Maximus. Crowe is a highly celebrated actor, who is respected by many people. Crowe's performances in films have elevated the industry of acting. So what better to do than merge his realities with his characters' fantasies?

Crowe was able to divide his fantasies from his realities and conquer them making him and Maximus one person. He didn't think of himself as Russell Crowe the Award Winning Actor, he became Maximus Decimus Meridius the Roman General. For this to work successfully, Crowe had to live within his own fantasy. He had to live in an illusion where he was an Army general whose wife was killed by a jealous tyrant on a rise to power. When Crowe began to believe this illusion everyone else did to… That is the power of good actors.

In order to be a good actor you have to sacrifice your sanity in order for the bigger purpose. The ends justify the means and acting is no different. An actor must believe their own… "Bullshit" in order to make other people believe. If an actor can do this, the ultimate illusion is achievable. When goods actors are placed together, you have the greatest example of illusion interruption… welcome to the movies.

A movie is a sequence of images projected onto a screen with sufficient rapidity to create the illusion of motion and continuity. A movie has the ability to captivate and control because a movie is a control within itself. If a movie cannot sustain the illusion that still pictures are moving then it becomes inadequate in effectiveness. The fact that a movie has the ability to create illusions is the reason why it has the power to control.

As stated earlier, when an illusion has the ability to make fantasy and reality ambiguous it also has the ability to divide and conquer. Ultimately an illusion controls everyone that believes in it. Disney movies present the biggest forms of illusion interruption. For this reason, Disney is one of the highest grossing production companies in the world. Disney understands how an illusion works. They understand that if they can take something from someone's fantasy and then apply it to real occurrence they can make the ultimate illusion, entertainment.

Entertainment holds the attention of people with something amusing or diverting. That is why people love it. Entertainment capitalizes on your fantasies to divert you from reality. Because you become entangled within this fantasy you no longer want go back to reality. In due time, you can longer tell the difference. When it's time to go back to reality, it is no longer accepted because you've been entertained with unstrained fancies. The ambiguity of real and fake allows you to accept illusion interruption.

Cartoons, for example, have the phenomenal power to entertain. The reason this exists is because it takes a concept that is not present in reality and puts it there. Finding Nemo, one of America's greatest triumphs as far as animation goes grossed $339,714,978 in America alone. Worldwide this movie grossed $864,625,978. That's a lot of clams!!! The effectiveness of this movie is because of illusion interruption. This movie made a world where fish were like people, and they had jobs according to their species and acted in the nature of their given names. To clarify my point Marlon, a clown fish, is constantly expected to tell jokes because of his species. The ironies in these situations often arise when expectations of humor from a clown fish is replaced with disappointment, because Marlon is unable to make other fish laugh.

The instances in the movie in which this happens evoke laughter. This is because we are all familiar with discrimination. There are times in our lives where because of our identities we are categorized and expected to behave a certain way. If we act accordingly to the person's assumptions they'll continue to accept it. But if our behavior doesn't correlate with the presumed expectancy then it distorts illusion interruption with reality intervention. Now the person knows that just because a person is assigned an identity doesn't mean that they'll act accordingly to the expected behavior. Finding Nemo was able to use discrimination satirically, because it showed that you shouldn't judge someone based on how they look.

In theory, that was one of the factors that made Finding Nemo a classic. It poked fun at how people expect one thing out of a person but see another. In addition, the result of the event leaves them confused. Kids are subconsciously transmitted this message and become less likely to judge because they have seen that everything is not as it seems. The movies' overall triumph is shown in the plot.

In the beginning of the movie, Marlon has a wife. He finds them a new house and they have hundreds of eggs waiting to be hatched. Amidst the rejoicing of their new home and future, a swordfish comes. The mother, in nature, attempts to prevent her babies from being eaten. Her sudden action to prevent the swordfish from eating her kids ironically leads to the death of her and all of the eggs. Marlon, being knocked unconscious, wakes up to find his wife and kids eaten. When he believes that all is lost, he finds one egg. Feeling guilty for allowing his wife and the rest of his kids to be killed, he vows to never allow anything to happen to his new egg Nemo.

A

d

As the movie progresses, there are countless situations in which Marlon is conflicted with allowing Nemo to do things. Because of Marlon's past, he forces Nemo to avoid all danger. This eventually leads to Nemo defying his father's demand of not touching a boat. As a result of Nemo's defiance, he is abducted by a scuba diver. The very thing that Marlon tried to prevent happens, something happened to Nemo.

In the relentless pursuit of his son, Marlon bumps into a fish named Dory. Dory, a fish who exhibits poor memory, decides to help him. When he decides to accept her help, she forgets she told him she would help. When he tries to leave her, he bumps into a shark named Bruce. Marlon, being scared since the death of his wife, is weary of sharks because he knows of their nature. Dory on the other hand, has no problem talking to sharks because of her inability to remember "fish etiquette."

Her unbiased actions lead to the revelation that Bruce and his shark friends were vegetarians. Marlon and Dory are attending a "Fish are Friends" seminar in which Marlon begins to learn the sincerity of the shark's intentions. When they are asked to introduce themselves, Marlon states that he is a clown fish. When the sharks hear this, they assume that he is funny so they ask him to tell a joke. Marlon's inadequacy of joke telling causes one of the sharks to say "Ya know for a clown fish, he's not that funny."

This shows how much prejudices are inherent are instilled within self-identity. In order for you to define yourself, you have to divide yourself from everyone else. To do this, you have to take a general action that everyone is capable of and apply it to someone directly. When this is done, awareness is promoted by rebuking the action that has been assigned to someone else. Division occurs between the two and the creator of the division now has an axis of power. But, in doing this there has to be a realization that you have now limited your capabilities. The only way you can divide someone else is if you divide yourself, the only way you can conquer someone else is if conquer yourself. People that limit others only limit themselves. Just because you think a person acts a certain way doesn't make it true. This is illusion interruption.

This segment of the movie once again reiterated discrimination. This scene illustrated the intricacies of self-identity in terms of illusion interruption. Marlon takes it offensive to have the assumption of being funny just because he's a clown fish. But when a shark comes around, he has no problem assuming that he will be eaten. Illusion interruption has ability to make fantasy and reality ambiguous, so when these concepts are shown separately there is utter confusion and duality in logic. So there's no problem when you are prejudice, but when a prejudiced is applied to you it becomes a problem. This is still illusion interruption.

… Marlon finds the goggles that fell off the scuba diver. Unfortunately, because he is a fish he is unable to read English. Dory, in her attempt to help, takes the goggles to Bruce for him to read. Marlon, still in a state of skepticism, doesn't want Bruce to help. Dory and Marlon begin to fight over the goggles. As a result, the goggles hit Dory in the nose causing her to bleed. The blood is inhaled by Bruce, making him crave fish. Bruce begins to pursue Dory and Marlon, in the midst of this Marlon learns that Dory can read English.

While Bruce is chasing them, his shark friends are trying to prevent him from eating Marlon and Dory. Because an expected outcome is present, Marlon sustains his belief that sharks still eat fish. However, Marlon neglects the reality that the other sharks are preventing Bruce from eating them. In addition he neglects to realize that if he had not prevented Dory from asking Bruce to help, they wouldn't have fought over the goggles consequently leading to Dory's nose bleed. The nose bleed is what triggered Bruce's reaction, but Bruce's reaction is a reflection of Marlon's ignorance. Marlon's inability to distinguish his fantasy from his reality leaves him confused. Because he remains confused, he remains in illusion interruption.

Nemo, being abducted by the scuba diver, is placed into a fish tank. While being there, he is introduced into a world that is unlike his. Although he was originally given mental boundaries stating that he couldn't do anything by his father, the concept of a physical boundary scared him even more. Nemo's separation from Marlon showed how Marlon's prevention of giving his son freedom led to the abduction by the scuba diver. The only reason why Nemo touched the boat was because his father told him that he was incapable of doing so. Nemo was born with a physical ailment; he had a little fin which made it seem harder for Nemo to be like other fish. When you mix the reality of Nemo's physical state and the guilt of Marlon's past you have another illusion interruption.

Marlon, seeing his sons' physical ailment and knowing his own, placed mental boundaries around his son. In making these boundaries, the original vow of not allowing anything happen to Nemo becomes self-fulfilling prophecy in which he now believes that Nemo in incapable of doing anything. In reality Nemo is just as capable as any other fish, but because he was always limited by his fathers' boundaries he only adapts the mindset that he couldn't do anything.

The mind and the body, like emotions, are similar to polarity. Because Nemo was fed an extreme image for so long, his body and mind begins to reject the extreme image with an opposite image. He was told all the things that he couldn't do and he listened. Because Nemo never challenged his father's authority, this fulfilled Marlon's prophecy of preventing anything from happening to him. This made them both mentally weak because they would now avoid things that they have no personal experience of dealing with things themselves.

When Marlon says to Nemo, "You think you can do all these things but you just can't, Nemo!!!" That extreme comment leads to the extreme opposite. He was told to not swim out in the open water and Nemo listened. When Marlon sees Nemo by the open water he assumes that Nemo is being defiant even when there's no actual proof. Nemo's reassurance of not going out into the open water is not met with admiration or reward but with distrust and hostility. Nemo, being conflicted between fantasy and reality, touches the boat to spite his father. This action was performed to show that he is capable doing things. This is an excellent example of the saying, "Cut off the nose to spite the face." Nemo, being the nose, risks his own safety to show his father, the face, that he shouldn't be underestimated. By risking his own safety he begins to destroy Marlon's illusion interruption with reality intervention.

It was Nemo's spiteful action which led to him being abducted. Once again because Marlon neglects the reality that his son is capable of swimming out into open water, it pushes Nemo into a corner which forces him to retaliate with the opposite: Newton's third law of motion. Marlon was infuriated by the Nemo's actions, not because Nemo did something bad but mainly because Nemo distorted his father's illusion. But when Nemo is abducted by the scuba diver, it reinstates Marlon's illusion interruption. Nemo's abduction shows Marlon just how inadequate Nemo's ability is to protect himself. So in order to retain his illusion, Marlon must retrieve his son.

The fish tank that Nemo is being held in has a physical boundary of four walls. Mix Nemo's mental ailment of being told he is incapable of doing things with the physical factor of having a small fin **and** being confined within a physical boundary: Nemo's in illusion interruption. Already frightened by the reflection of his mental mind state becoming a physical obstacle, he becomes even more frightened when he meets the other fish that live in the tank. Because these fish are physically different, it frightens him. The reason he is frightened is because he has never experienced diversity before, because he was always told to avoid it. In doing this, Nemo ends up being stuck in the filter. He asks for help, his first sign of illusion interruption dependency. When the fish attempt to help him, a fish named Gill tells them to leave him alone. Gill then tells Nemo to swim out of the filter. Nemo, always being restricted by his father, tells Gill he has a small fin and is unable to do it.

Gill tells Nemo "It never stopped me…" and shows Nemo his damaged fin. When Nemo sees this, it disrupts his illusion interruption with reality interruption. Because an element of illusion interruption is broken, Nemo now gets himself out of the filter. Nemo, feeling triumphant, has now broken a mental boundary by defying a physical situation. He begins to meet all of the fish that are in the fish tank.

What's significant about the scuba divers tank is the diversity of the fish tank. None of the fish are physically alike, but it's their mental will for physical freedom which unites them. Realistically, if you put too many different species of fish into one tank they'll kill each other off. But, the movie shows how the physical appearance of the fish doesn't divide them but only makes them stronger. Because each fish is physically different, they contribute something that another fish needs mentally. For example Peach, the starfish, uses her ability of sticking to surfaces to be the tank lookout. Jacque, the shrimp, uses his bottom-feeding ability to cleanse the fish from the sea.

...Impressed with Nemo's ability to perform tasks in the face of adversity, he initiates him into their "Tank Gang." His new name "Shark-Bait" represents his new mental freedom. The plan for the Tank Gang is to escape the tank and get back into the ocean where they belong. They use Nemo's physical "weakness" of him being small to uplift his mental power by giving him the most important job of clogging the filter. What this will do is cause the fish tank to get dirty, so dirty it will force the scuba diver to clean it. When the fish are placed in individual baggies, they will roll out the window and across the street into the nearby river.

When the plan is put into effect it doesn't go quite as expected. Nemo was able to fit into the filter and place the rock into the rotator. Ironically, the rock is too small to successfully jam the rotator. Nemo, swimming out of the filter, is sucked back in! The Tank Gang rescues him by using teamwork, but because Nemo was unable to perform the task he was recaptured by illusion interruption. He began to believe that his physical appearance contributed to his failure, believing that his father was right all along. Nemo, feeling mentally distraught, begins to retract to his mental state of illusion interruption dependency.

Marlon and Dory survive the shark attack, but the goggles fall into the darkest depth of the sea. Marlon, once again being scared, allows illusion interruption to get the best of him. He is unable to pursue the only link to his son because of the fear that his past will resurface. This part shows the dangers of dividing and conquering, Marlon's limitation on his son reflects the limitation that he placed on himself. It is shown here that the only person controlled by illusion interruption is Marlon. Dory continues to swim challenging Marlon's illusion of being afraid of the dark. She continues to swim down to the depths of the sea singing "Just keep swimming; just keep swimming, what we do? We swim, swim, and swim," this song is a response to Marlon's pessimism. Confused by the logic of the statement he follows Dory ironically singing the song to that causes him to overcome his fear of the dark. Dory's song represents reality intervention because it shows that the present is the only thing to consider, the past can't be changed so why cry over spilled milk?

That is the hardest thing to accept, the past will remain in the past. The attempt to prevent the past only makes it happen quicker. If you stay focused on the past, you will always mentally live in the past regardless of your present physical state. Applying the past to the present is illusion interruption, focusing on the present is reality intervention. Due to Dory's words of wisdom, Marlon is able to now continue the task of finding his son.

While Marlon and Dory are swimming amidst the depths of the briny deep, Marlon accidentally touches Dory causing her to scream. Due to poor memory she asks if Marlon is her conscious. Marlon says "Yes, we haven't spoken in a while." This line shows the continuing conflict of illusion interruption. Marlon's illusion is distorted by Dory's actions. Fish are supposed to be scared of...everything. But this fish who cannot remember anything seems not be phased by any precedent set by nature.

When they see a light, they are intrigued by the beauty of it. For once since the beginning of the movie, Marlon does not question the nature of his present happiness. What they end up learning is that this object of beauty is connected to something that wants to eat them. While being chased by this fish, Marlon and Dory find the goggles that fell on a rock. Because Dory is the only one who can read English, Marlon has to distract the fish. However, it becomes hard when he has to get the fish to bring its light by the goggles so Dory can read them.

Forgetting about his past fear, Dory is able to read the goggles. When Marlon asks Dory what the goggles said, she was able to remember. Fascinated with her ability to remember, she begins to repeat it constantly. Because Dory forgot about her poor memory, she was able to remember what the goggles said. This shows Dory's own contemplation with illusion interruption. Her inability to remember allows her to maneuver through the sea without fear; ironically this inability is what helps Marlon. When she first meets Marlon she tells him that she suffer from short-term memory loss. However, throughout the movie she forgets her own doctrine which helps her to remember.

While swimming, Marlon decides that because he has the location of his son he no longer needs Dory. When Marlon tells her this, she is unable to accept this. Her inability to accept this reflects Marlon's inability to be confrontational. When Marlon makes statements towards leaving her, it is his own illusion interruption of being non-confrontational that hinders his ability to get his point across. Marlon says something, based on Dory's reactions he rebukes it to replace it with something else only confusing Dory further. Her confusion only reflects Marlon's state of guilt. When groups of fish come to comfort Dory, Marlon tries to ease the situation but it's already too late. The fish, not liking Marlon, amuse Dory with a game of charades. Marlon, being mocked by the fish, decides to leave.

Dory asks the fish if they know how to get to Sydney. Dory is given the directions, but the fish give Dory a fatal warning, when they come across a trench they have to swim through it not over it. When they reach the trench Marlon, being frightened by the appearance of the trench, wants to go over. Dory, remembering what the fish told her, tells him that they should swim through. Marlon, still in illusion interruption, insists that they swim over. Dory doesn't want to swim over because she remembers that they were supposed to swim through.

So Marlon decides to play on Dory's optimism to get her swim over the trench.

Once they're over the trench, they are surrounded by Jelly-fish! Dory, not being frightened by anything, is playing on top of the Jelly-fish. Marlon, never encountering a Jelly-fish, is frightened by Dory's "ignorance." Ironically it is her "ignorance" that exposes Marlon's. Marlon decides to make a game where they bounce on the Jelly-fish tops to get out of the Jelly-fish field. When Marlon makes it out he realizes that Dory is no longer with him. Feeling guilty by his manipulation of Dory's sincerity and optimism, he goes back to find her.

He sees her laying unconscious on the top of a Jelly-fish. He risks his life to save Dory, and because he was able to focus primarily on the present he saves her. Another illusion interruption has just been broken. Every time Marlon is faced with a clear and present danger, he forgets his illusion interruption and overcomes his past fear. Ironically because he doesn't see it this way, he still remains in illusion interruption.

Marlon and Dory, both being knocked unconscious, are retrieved by a group of Green Sea Turtles. When Marlon wakes up, he is greeted by Crush. In a state of panic, he looks for Dory. Seeing her scar, Marlon continues to exhibit more guilt. Dory, lying down, pops up and plays and seek with the younger Sea Turtles. Relieved, Marlon begins to talk to Crush. Crush begins to relay to Marlon the events that transpired. Crush, a turtle who represents mental freedom, commends Marlon on his bravery by swimming through Jelly-Fish field.

When Crush's son Squirt swims out of the current, Marlon rushes out to his safety. Crush immediately stops him; confused by this, Marlon questions Crush's logic. Crush tells Marlon that you have to allow people to do things for themselves or they'll never learn. Crush then tells him the nature of Green Sea Turtles. He tells Marlon that when Sea Turtles are born, they are left to hatch by themselves. When hatched, the eggs find their way back to their parents. Marlon, wanting an explanation, asks Crush how he knows when the kids are ready. Even in his uncertainty, Crush is still able to understand the logic behind the statement "Well you never but when they know, you know, you know?"

Life is like Crush's statement. You never actually know what to expect, so you begin to expect everything. But when you expect everything, you do nothing. All this process does is sends you into a circle that is unable to be followed. Because people expect things to be done for them, they end up doing nothing because they have expectations of everything happening to them. For this reason, you begin to neglect the reality of experiencing everything, because you are expecting something different. But when you don't know what to expect, you start to experience everything because you start to appreciate all of the experiences you've had, not with regret but with satisfaction.

When Squirt returns from the current, Marlon learns something. His illusion interruption now starts to become distorted with reality intervention. This is the first time that Marlon actually begins to understand life for what it is. He starts to see that the past controls the present, but this can only occur if you allow it to. When Squirt asks what happened to his son, Marlon begins to explain the story. Although Marlon doesn't see all the obstacles he and Dory have overcome as spectacular, this story now becomes the greatest story across the sea.

Being passed from fish to fish, the story becomes a legend. Like all stories, when they are repeated too much, they begin to lose meaning. So to keep the qualities that excite and stimulate, extra details must be added to the story. This story, which is originally explained in reality intervention, in due time becomes illusion interruption. By the time this story reaches the Australian harbor, Marlon becomes the most celebrated fish in the ocean!

Nemo, feeling distraught from his past failure, confines himself to solitude. As life has it Nigel, a Pelican, looks for Nemo to tell him the fantastic story of his father. When Nigel begins to tell him the story, Nemo is in a state of skepticism due to his conflict with illusion interruption. But when Nigel is able to explain that his father is the clown fish from the reef, Nemo becomes ecstatic. Hearing how his father "fought" three sharks, sea monsters, Jelly-fish, and rode a fleet of Green Sea Turtles, breaks Nemo's conflict of illusion interruption.

Because Nemo has seen his father overcome every fear, Nemo know breaks his illusion interruption with reality intervention. Nemo, no longer worrying about the past, finds a rock and overcomes his fear of the filter. The Tank Gang, scared for his life, tells him not to do it. But by the time they can stop him, Nemo has already completed the task. The conquering of Nemo's illusion interruption shows the reflection of Marlon's. Because Nemo heard the story of his father conquering everything he was made to fear, Nemo can now overcome his fear of the filter. In order for you to control the present, you must rebuke the future. If Nemo would've never heard the story of his father's bravery, Nemo would've never become brave either. In order to break illusion interruption, the person or thing that first instills it within you must break theirs as well.

Marlon and Dory now being let off by the Sea Turtles, continue the journey of finding Nemo. They ride the East Australian Current, because that is the passage that leads to Sydney. Before getting on the current, Squirt gives them proper exiting technique. Unable to hear him, Marlon is forced to expect nothing. In result, Marlon begins to appreciate the experience more because he had no forethought of it. Before Crush leaves, Marlon remembers that he told Nemo if he ever met a Sea Turtle he would ask him his age. What was originally said sarcastically to Nemo now becomes sincere. When Marlon told Nemo he would find out how old Sea Turtles are, he had no intentions of ever meeting a Sea Turtle. Ironically, he is pushed into a situation where he actually finds out how old a Sea Turtle is. This irony shows the effects of self-fulfilling prophecy.

A self-fulfilling prophecy, the way sociologist Robert K. Merton explains it, is initially a false definition of a situation evoking a new behavior which makes the once false statement become true. Marlon's sarcasm towards Nemo showed a division in their relationship. People use sarcasm when they want to ridicule or inflict pain to someone.

What's effective about sarcasm is its ability to dish out pain indirectly. Sarcasm plays on the fault of a personal flaw to expose someone else's. So Marlon's claim to find out how old Sea Turtles are poked fun at his flaw of being afraid of everything, but also pokes fun at Nemo's naivety.

But Marlon's sarcasm became his own self-fulfilling prophecy. So the ridicule of his own flaw inadvertently causes Marlon to change his own behavior, thus making the sarcastic statement of meeting a Sea turtle true. But it is noteworthy to know that this only transpired due to the statement originally being false... Crush tells Marlon that he is "150 years old, and still young." This showed Marlon that age was a mind state, not a physical boundary. With another level of illusion interruption being distorted with reality intervention, Marlon and Dory now continue towards Sydney.

As Marlon and Dory are swimming, Marlon begins to realize that they're swimming in circles. Before illusion interruption begins to capture Marlon again, Dory intervenes with reality telling him to calm down and ask for help. Marlon, unable to understand the logic behind Dory's statement, allows her to prove herself. Dory, becoming her own self-fulfilling prophecy, finds a whale. She tells Marlon that she can speak whale, but Marlon still conflicted with illusion intervention, is unable to accept this. So instead of trying to convince him, Dory begins to speak whale.

When Dory begins to speak whale, Marlon's skepticism tries to limit Dory's ability. Dory, now being influenced by Marlon, rebukes her last action by saying she was speaking the wrong dialect. Marlon, fearing that Dory's carelessness will cause something bad to happen, tells her to stop. Once again, because Marlon tries to prevent something, it only happens quicker... They're eaten by the whale. While being in the whale's mouth, Dory is doing what she does best: Just keep swimming. Marlon on the other hand, is now recaptured by illusion interruption. He is back in a state of confusion and displacement. Feeling pushed to an extreme, he breaks down.

Dory, feeling for Marlon, consoles him by telling him that everything is going to be okay. Because Dory says this, she again becomes her own self-fulfilling prophecy. She decides to speak whale to get them out of the same situation that she has placed them in. Believing that it was Dory's fault for their current predicament, he tells her to stop. She reassures him that she is capable of this task, but in Marlon's frustration he screams out something that shows just how strong his conflict is with illusion interruption. "You think you can do all of these things, but you just can't Nemo!!!"

At this juncture in the movie, Marlon realizes his problem. It was never about Dory, it was his unresolved issue with his son. This is when he explains his frustrations saying "I promised Nemo that I would never allow anything to happen to him." **Dory replies** "Well if you didn't allow anything to happen to him, then nothing would ever happen to him." **Suddenly, the whale begins to swallow the** water in its mouth. In a state of panic, Marlon says "It's half empty!" **Dory replies** "Hmm, it looks half full." Frustrated at the optimism that he is unable to achieve, he tells Dory to stop it. As the water is digested, Marlon hangs on to the whale's tongue. Dory, understanding whale, says "Okay" and jumps. Marlon, unable to understand the logic of Dory's action, grabs her fin. She tells him "It is time to let go." After, Dory then tells Marlon to trust her.

Initially, Marlon finds this hard but when he looks at the scar on Dory's body, he remembers that the scar on her body came from her ability to trust him. Dory reiterates that everything will be okay. Looking for reassurance, Marlon asks how she knows. Dory, being completely honest, says "I don't know." Being left no other choice, Marlon decides to let go. When they let go, Marlon and Dory are blown out of the whale's hole. Being freed from another state of illusion interruption, Marlon now believes that he too can speak whale. Ironically, Dory says to Marlon "I didn't know you can speak whale." The same limitation that Marlon placed on Dory's ability to speak whale is coherent in Dory's statement of Marlon speaking whale.

As stated earlier, the only way you can make trap someone within illusion interruption is if you believe the illusion yourself. Marlon's belief that Dory couldn't speak whale ultimately led to Dory believing Marlon. Consequently leading to Dory's shock when Marlon is able to speak the same language in which she was told she could not do.

…Marlon and Dory's quest to find Nemo continues when they look up to find out that they are in Sydney. When they come to the surface to see where they are, a Pelican comes and snatches them from out of the water. Marlon, on the verge of being eaten, decides that he has come too far to be breakfast. Ironically, it is past experiences that lead him to his present decision of not being eaten. To Marlon, he feels that he has overcome worst fears and this is no different. When reality intervention is introduced yet again, he clogs the Pelicans' throat causing him to choke.

Nigel, laughing at the Pelican for choking, decides to help him. When Nigel approaches the Pelican, he asks "What's wrong, cat got your tongue?" This forces the pelican to expose Marlon and Dory. Seeing Dory and Marlon, and remembering the countless stories of his bravery, causes Nigel to want to help. When Marlon and Dory fall onto an open dock they try to get back into the water. Nigel, trying to help, chases them down. When Marlon and Dory hit the docks' corner, they are surrounded by pigeons. Nigel, finally able to catch up to them tells him that if they want to live they have to get in his mouth. Uncouthness surrounds Marlon, forcing him to try to escape further.

But when Nigel tells him that he knows his son Nemo, Marlon's reaction triggers a wild chase where Nigel takes Marlon and Dory to Nemo. Being chased by pigeons, Nigel now makes it to the dentist office where Nemo is being held captive…

Nemo, on the verge of being given to the scuba divers' niece Darla, has made the tank dirty. It is in Jacque the shrimps' nature to clean, so when the tank gets dirty he finds it hard to resist the urge to clean. This is another phenomenal example of illusion interruption. The Tank Gang made a vow to make the tank dirty so that the plan can work effectively.

But, it conflicts with Jacques nature to clean. So much so, Jacque is caught trying to clean a section of the tank. This illustrates how the strains of illusion interruption conflicts with reality intervention. The past will always conflict with the present, thus influencing the future.

If Jacque was not forced to stop cleaning, his illusion interruption would've destroyed the plan of getting Nemo back to his father… While sleeping, the scuba diver (who is now the dentist) cleans the tank with a new type of filter. This filter, better than the last, is unable to be clogged. The advancement in the filters' technology discourages the Tank Gang, but it discourages Nemo far more because it forces him to think that he will never see his father again.

Darla, the dentists' niece, is a girl who in excitement of liking fish kills them. Nemo's sole purpose for being abducted was to please the fancies of Darla. Excuse the digression… Because all of the fish lived in the dentist's office for so long, they begin to pick up the trade of dentistry. They knew what every tool was called, the techniques that dentists used, they even debated on what caused cavities. Being exposed to something for so long causes you to adapt. In doing so, you no longer feel threatened by it…

Darla, a girl who looks obnoxious in appearance, comes to get Nemo. Her obnoxious appearance reflects her obnoxious illusion interruption. When the dentist tries to put Nemo in the net, he is unable to escape. Gill and the Tank Gang all dive into the net sacrificing their own livelihood for the Nemo. This action shows the importance of a team. A team is not based on the individual; it is based on the group. Although individuality is appreciated in a team due to the diversity it brings, it is ultimately the combination of the groups' diversity which makes them stronger. Because all of the fish were able to able to equally produce one action, they were able to help Nemo.

Unfortunately, their extreme action of unity pushes the dentist to an opposite extreme of division. Waiting for Nemo to be alone, the dentist captures Nemo with a fish baggie. When is placed onto the counter, he attempts to roll out of the window. The dentist, able to catch him before he rolls out, places him on a metal plate. When Darla comes in, the dentist tells Darla that he got her a fish. Overwhelmed with the news, Darla grabs the baggie and looks at Nemo. Darla's illusion interruption surfaces with her affinity for shaking fish baggies. Darla shakes fish baggies to wake them up; ironically it is this same action that ends up putting them to sleep forever. Lol!!! I'm sorry, but that is too funny.

Darla never realizes this so she always ends up killing her fish. Nemo, knowing Darla's nature is able to adapt by playing dead. Playing dead, a defense mechanism used by many animals… and humans, is one the most effective tools for survival. When you play dead, you put yourself into a state of total vulnerability. Although this may seem stupid to some, the extreme state of vulnerability causes the predator to respond with the extreme opposite of vulnerability. Unwilling to devour their prey, the predator leaves the prey alone. Tell me this isn't satire at its best? Damn I'm good!!!

Darla, now believing that she has killed the fish, begins to cry. The Tank Gang, looking at Nemo's physical state of immobility, Darla's reaction, and their knowledge of her treatment with fish begin to exhibit dismay. Nemo has just placed the Tank Gang into illusion interruption. When Nemo winks at them, the Tank Gang's illusion interruption is broken with reality intervention. When the dentist comes into the room, he sees that Nemo is dead and Darla is crying.

At this exact time, Marlon, Nigel and Dory come into the dentist office to get Nemo. When Marlon sees Nemo, he is destroyed by Nemo's current appearance. Believing that Nemo is dead destroys his illusion interruption. When the dentist is able to wrestle Nigel out of the office, Nigel, placing both Dory and Marlon back into the water, apologizes for his son's lost. No longer believing in either reality intervention and illusion interruption, Marlon becomes totally disconnected and displaced, ultimately leading to his insanity.

This insanity causes him to rebuke the person who has helped him get so far, Dory. When Dory begins to explain that he cannot leave saying that "I don't want to forget anymore, I can remember things when I look at you, because when I look at you I'm home." **Marlon replies saying** "Well I want to forget."

Dory and Marlon's relationship throughout the movie summarizes the relationship of illusion interruption and reality intervention. Marlon reflects illusion interruption because he uses past conflicts to control the future. When he does this, it makes him oblivious to the present, resulting in déjà vu. This causes his sanity to be trapped in illusion interruption. So everything he dislikes in himself he dislikes in other fish. However because he is unable to accept his present mind state, different situations which do not correlate with illusion interruption always leaves him dazed and confused. Because Marlon expects everything to happen, nothing happens.

Dory however represents reality intervention, because she knows nothing of the past. Because of this, she is always forced to experience things for herself. Ironically, it is her ability to forget which enables her to always treat other fish equally. Because she is never focused on the past she is rarely concerned with the future. As a result, she always stays in the reality intervention; she always stays in the present. This may seem dangerous, but it is this same danger that keeps her safe. Dory is able to maneuver through the ocean assimilating to every culture that she encounters, making her the most lovable character in the movie. "When in Rome, Do what the Romans do." **Dory expects nothing, so she experiences everything.**

However it is the combination of both concepts which lead to the greater purpose, Finding Nemo. If Marlon would've never met Dory, he would've never been able to conquer his fears. Likewise with Dory; if she hadn't met Marlon, she would have never been able to remember the address to where Nemo was. It should now be understood that this within itself is illusion interruption.

Nemo, believed to be dead, is taken by the dentist and is taken towards the garbage. In efforts to fulfill his promise, Gill once again sacrifices his own livelihood to save Nemo. Because the dentist loves his fish, he neglects his past action with a new action; he tries to save Gill by placing him back into the fish tank. This scene illustrates the dentists' illusion interruption. Because he loves his fish, he neglects the present action of throwing Nemo into the garbage in order to save the future idea that one of his fish will die.

Gill uses the metal plate as a sea saw to pop Nemo into the sink. The dentist makes it just in time to save Gill. Gill tells the Tank Gang "All drains lead to the sea." This quote is one of symbolic freedom. The sea is a symbolism of freedom because it is never-ending and ever flowing. The sea, being a physical representation of freedom, is only for those who have no mental boundaries. Nemo breaks all of his mental boundaries by overcoming illusion interruption; because of this, he is able to have the ultimate physical representation of freedom, the sea.

When Nemo is reintroduced back into the sea, he has a new mind state. His new found freedom allows him to find Dory. When he meets Dory, he notices that she is lost (being that Marlon was her physical representation for consciousness and memory). Nemo, now losing all of his past convictions, tells Dory that they can help each other find who they lost. When Dory asks Nemo his name he tells her. Because Dory is no longer around Marlon, she forgets who Nemo is. Throughout the movie, she continually forgets Nemo's name. Although she forgets his name, she continues to help Marlon find Nemo.

While Dory and Nemo are swimming, she reads a pipe that says Sydney. When she reads this, her memory is suddenly restored. Being able finally remember Nemo, she is glad to find. Once again, it is Dory's inability to remember which helps her break the illusion interruption that she can't remember. Because Dory stays in reality intervention, she is always able to adapt. Now having Nemo, they begin to look for Marlon. In the midst of looking for him, they see two crabs that've seen him earlier. When Dory asks if they know where he went. The crab responds "Yea I seen him, but I'm not telling you and there's nothing you can do about it."

Hearing that, Dory is given an extreme response forcing her to respond with an extreme opposite. She knows that crabs fear being eaten by birds so she uses the crabs fear to her advantage. She puts him above the water for the pigeons to eat him. The crab, being scared of pigeons, decides to talk. When Dory and Nemo find Marlon, Marlon is ecstatic. While they're rejoicing for their reunion, a group of fishermen cast a net into the area that they're in.

Marlon, scared to lose his son again, he's able to save Nemo from the net. Unfortunately, Dory is caught in the net! Nemo, remembering the tactic used by the Tank Gang, swims into the net. Marlon, seeing his worst nightmare repeat itself, tells Nemo to not do it. Nemo tells his father "It's the only way to save Dory." Considering the past, Marlon allows Nemo to prove himself.

Nemo tells all of the fish swim down at the same time. The fish, all swimming in different directions, begin to all swim down in unison. This forces the net to be weighed down by the enormous force of teamwork. When the net is finally broken, all the fish are freed. But Nemo is lying at the bottom of the sea floor appearing hurt. Marlon rushes down to see if he's alright. Although he initially appears hurt, Nemo is able to wake up. Relieved to get his son back, Marlon tells Nemo that Sea Turtles live to be 150 years old. Confused by this, Nemo tells Marlon that, "But Sandy Plankton said they only live to be one hundred?"

Marlon tells Nemo, "Sandy Plankton? Do you think I swam all the way across the ocean and not know more than Sandy Plankton?" In the beginning of the movie, Nemo tells his father all of the things Sandy told him. Nemo talks about meeting a shark, Sea Turtles and many other creatures that inhabit the sea. Although Sandy Plankton in never actually shown in the movie, Nemo takes Sandy Plankton's words as dogmatic. 'Sandy Plankton" is a symbolic character in the movie. Her first name, "Sandy" is a representation of the sand, representing her ability to be everywhere at the same time. Her last name being "Plankton" representing the living organism that travels throughout the ocean. The combination of these names makes everything that Sandy says sound believable. So when Nemo debates the age of Sea Turtles with his father, it reflects his own illusion interruption of believing people just because of their characteristics.

Sandy Plankton illustrated the idea of how rumors are spread. They never show Sandy Plankton, but because her name is inherent within sea life, she is easily believed. No one knows how rumors start; ironically, people tend to follow them. So when Marlon makes that statement about the age of a Green Sea Turtle, this conflicts with Nemo's illusion interruption of being naïve. However, it is Nemo's naivety which builds the plot for the movie. If Nemo hadn't repeated what Sandy Plankton said, then Marlon would've never made the sarcastic comments of meeting a shark and asking a Sea Turtle's their name. This sarcasm became self-fulfilling prophecy because he had to disprove Sandy Plankton's illusion interruption by experiencing these things for himself.

Ironically, Marlon telling his son how old Sea Turtles are becomes another illusion interruption because Nemo will believe his father just because he swam across the ocean. At the end of the movie, Marlon is able to tell a funny joke. Thinking about Marlon's past, they find it hard to believe that he fought a shark. Just then, Bruce and his other shark friends drop Dory off from another Fish are Friends meeting. Now having actual proof, Marlon's friends believe him. The situation where Marlon tells a joke is a great example of reality intervention and illusion interruption. When the group of fish first meets Marlon they assume that he's funny. This assumption leads to disappointment. However, at the end of the movie, the groups' conflict with illusion interruption of Marlon not being funny is distorted with the reality intervention of Marlon being funnier than before.

In a bonus scene, the dentist is shown cleaning the tank. When he looks for the fish that he placed in individual baggies, they are able to make it to the river. Once the last member of the Tank Gang makes it into the water, they begin to celebrate. Not knowing what to do next, the Blowfish asks "Now what?"

This scene summarized my argument about illusion interruption and reality intervention. Because the Tank Gang assimilated to the dentists' environment, all they knew was dentistry. What originally was different and unusual became normal to them. So when they are finally able to make out into the sea, they are confused. Because they've been around dentistry for so long they've become "institutionalized." So regardless of their physical state, it is their mental that keeps illusion interruption. Moreover, because they are still in the plastic Baggies, it restrains their physical fancies of being free.

In result, this movie boosted the tourist attraction in Sydney, Australia. Tourists were snorkeling all for that chance to "Find Nemo." Petland Discounts probably held Blue Tangs and Clown Fish, but actually **Finding Nemo** makes all the difference. That's the power of entertainment.

Illusion Interruption is something like a Self-Fulfilling prophecy; it's not there until someone puts it there. I've explained Illusion Interruption in movies, now it's time for a challenge. I'll use it to explain this dreaded "Recession" we're going through. People say this word and have no idea what the fuck it means. Recession means to withdraw, to take back, a period of reduced economic activity. A Recession basically means to go back. If a "Recession" is real then I'm sure you can explain the multi-million dollar Condos being built everywhere. Condos weren't around during the Panic of 1837. Niggas are buying HDTVs. Hi-definition wasn't around during Black Tuesday. Unemployment hit 7%, but it didn't hit 10% like 1981. So is this market really going back, or is everyone just looking the wrong way? Let's find out.

Now when Robert K. Merton, the founder of Self-Fulfilling Prophecy Inc., discovered how his corporation worked, he explained so that niggas could understand the power of speculation and how effective a rumor is. This "recession" is nothing more than a self-fulfilling prophecy. Now I'm expecting to be hit with *facts* that are in *books* by *educated* people who feel I'm being ignorant and stupid. So let's get the *facts* about facts first, then I'll go on to explain how SFP Inc. "Serves and Protect" its citizens.

A Greek philosopher by the name of Protagoras held the statement saying that "Man is the measure of what exists." Followed by him came another man named Gorgias who took an even bolder step to say "Nothing exists; Even if something exists, nothing can be known about it; and Even if something can be known about it, knowledge about it can't be communicated to others." These two men became known as Sophists for their complicated way of thinking, nothing way black and white with these niggas everything was grey (I hope they didn't catch it). The terms' root is seen the word sophisticated. You know like the "sophisticated" niggas you see on TV that speculate about what exists in the market and what doesn't. Now if these sophisticated gentlemen say "recession" everything freezes, but if these same sophisticated gentlemen say "prosperity" then everything returns back to normal. Maybe I'm being too philosophical myself, let's do it as simple as possible for the educated people.

A fact is something that can be proven. A fact can be proven, a fact has actuality. So facts tend to be based on proof, correct? If I can't prove it, then it never happened right? Some of you may see a rhetorical fallacy in my argument but I'm not arguing, I'm *proving* a *fact*. Facts are found everywhere, in books, in libraries, in science, in religion, at your job, on the internet on the news on your walk to the corner store; facts are actuality, because facts can be proven, no matter what you do to a fact, a fact will remain a fact. So let's see how far this fact thing goes.

People cannot fly because of gravity, correct? There is proof that gravity exists, so according to the laws of gravity people can't fly. Galileo Galilei made some of the first assertions that gravity existed, Sir Isaac Newton followed this notion and furthered the study of gravity with *Principia*, and Albert Einstein even put his two cents in about gravity. These occurrences are all facts, but the only opinion in this fact seems to be gravity itself. Galileo made the claim about gravity in the 1600s, so would it be safe to say that people could fly in 1492? Maybe Christopher Columbus never sailed on the Santa Maria; he probably flew to the New World.

Another fact. Prior to 1973, in the DSM-I homosexuality was listed as a mental illness. So if you were homosexual in the 50s they sent you to a psychiatric hospital, because you were crazy for liking the same sex. This is a fact. And homosexuality being a mental sickness was a fact prior to 1973. Wait I have one more! It was a fact that women could never equate the contributions of a man. If a woman strived for equality she was a witch, not a figurative witch, an actual witch. In stories witches flew on brooms, brewed secret potions and kidnapped children. These witches were worse than any other fairy tale. In a time where Puritanical patriarchs ruled the world, their worst nightmare was a witch. Not a witch who could fly, or make secret potions. A witch was a woman who was displayed the same intelligence as a man. Females weren't supposed to be educated, so if a woman could read then the devil taught her, because there is no way a woman should ever equate a man. You know what Puritans did to the first Suffrage movement? Drowned it." If you were to float you were a witch and if you sank... you died."

That is a hell of a decision for a woman. You know why Puritans found nothing wrong with? Because it was in the bible, it's a fact. Illusion interruption.

"Get your facts first, and then you can distort them as much as you please"

A fact is what the majority believes. If everyone believes in it, people will go out and make a culture that reflects it. When you have a culture that reflects a belief, you now have proof. Now that I have enraged the educated, back to explaining how SFP Inc. will save you from the dreaded Boogey Man a.k.a. Recession. SFP Inc. specializes in telling you how a self-fulfilling prophecy works. First something is said that can't be proven. Because it can't be proven people try to disprove an unproven thing. In their attempts to disprove an unproven thing, they expedite the occurrence even quicker, and then the very thing that you said would happen does happen. Self-fulfilling prophecy.

Merton describes the power of speculation by using the parable of Millingville Bank. During a regular day in the bank, a lot of people come into the bank one day. Because this is a bank that is not necessarily crowded it leads some of the customers to worry. People begin to speculate about the bank the reason as to why this crowd has gathered so quickly. Because there is never a clear reason as to why this abnormal occurrence transpires, it leads to speculation. This speculation makes the assertion that the bank must be going insolvent, so that's why so many people are coming. As word gets out, more people begin to see the crowd and start to believe that the assertion is true. As people begin to all take their money out the bank, the bank begins to lose money and by the end of the day, the bank becomes insolvent. This all started with the speculation about an abnormal occurrence, which led to the once false statement becoming true.

"The parable tells us that public definitions of a situation (prophecies or predictions) become an integral part of the situation and thus affect subsequent developments, This is peculiar to human affairs. It is not found in the world of nature, untouched by human hands. Predictions of the return of Halley's Comet do not influence its orbit. But the rumored insolvency of Millingville's bank did affect the actual outcome. The prophecy of collapse led to its own fulfillment."

Self-Fulfilling prophecies works as stated, A says something that can't be proven. Instead of trying to prove their point they allow the statement to stand on its own. Because nothing exists without friction or opposition, the person hearing the statement will first ask A for the reason of their statement. Because A never gives a "logical" reason, B will go gets facts and try to disprove A's statement. While B gets their facts, they start to see that A's illogical statement had more clout than recognized. What B will now do is do whatever A tells them. Speculation tends to describe the financial term for the people who predict and guess whether a product or commodity will have profitability without actual proof. So often buying and selling stock is like playing craps. No one knows if they'll lose, no one will know if they'll lose so it depends on those who stick it out. In the business world it's not called gambling, that word is too unprofessional. So for the sake of prestige I'll say investment.

In terms of Speculative fever, people tend to talk about the profitability of an estate without having little to intention to ever live there. So what happens is people buy houses with the sole purpose to sell it back for a profit. Although it is quite risky, seeing that there is no actual proof as to whether the house will actually sell, people still do it. Now this financial "crisis" like past crises are noted when the housing market fails. When the housing market is bad, people tend to buy when it's cheap so that when the market is healthy again they can sell. This leads to profitability for the buyer. But this is only when the housing market goes from recession to prosperity. However, if someone buys a house when the market is healthy then the market goes bad, they're stuck with a house they had no intention on living in. But they can't sell it because they would lose their money, so they keep it in hopes that the market gets better.

If the market takes longer than expected, then the person crapped out. Mortgage statements are sent, but because the person never had an intention on living in the house, they don't pay the mortgage, because they don't pay for the house the house in foreclosed on. Not only has the bank crapped out, but the bank craps out 10 xs over, because the mortgage is never paid the bank loses money. Because the bank loses money they have to tighten the load and stricken the credit approvals. Because the housing market and credit lending go back like spinal cords and car seats, if you infringe one you threaten the other. So what happens is, the next time someone wants to buy a house, if they're credit isn't good, they will be denied a loan for the home. If this continues to persist then the housing market will continue to plummet because no one can afford a home right off the bat. So as the market continues to fail, the speculation gets worse and people begin to get their houses foreclosed on because they never had any intention on living there, it was an investment.

What this does is destroy the chances for people who actually want a home to live in. Because other people played craps and lost, it suffocates the chances of people who are actually sincere about owning a home. Because no one wants to take that risk of having their homes foreclosed on they tend to rent apartments as oppose to buying homes. So what tends to happen is rural areas begin to get deserted to grasp affordable living in cities, when cities become over-crowded, crime rises. Illusion interruption is the new Self-Fulfilling Prophecy.

"It's funny. All you have to do is say something nobody understands and they'll do practically anything you want them to."

Now, what Sophists do is take something that doesn't exist and makes it exist. For example, a recession is understood as a time of financial hardship. So whenever people hear "recession," they don't go out as much. Because people don't go out as much, stores don't make as much money. Because stores don't make as much money, they have to fire people. Because they have to fire people, they have to close down their stores. Because they have to close down their stores, unemployment rises. Because unemployment rises, depression rises. Because depression rises, people turn to drugs. Because people turn to drugs, crime rises. Because crime rises, police protection rises.

Now this usually 'll last until Sophists say the word "prosperity" or "the recession is over." Then people go out more, because people go out more, stores make more money. Because stores make money, stores can hire more employees, because stores can hire more employees, they can open more stores, because they can open more stores, unemployment declines. Because unemployment declines, depression declines, because depression declines, people turn away from drugs, because people turn away from drugs, crime decreases, because crime decreases, police decrease.

Example, when the Great Depression occurred, Herbert Hoover ain't do nothing about the problem. People were living on the street, people were dying of malaria, and people were selling liquor because that seemed to be the only way of a steady income. "Boot-legging" was the only way to make a fast buck on the streets, if you lived in America during this time, then the thing to be was a "boot-legger." Boot-leggers like Bugsy Siegel, Meyer Lansky, Al Capone, and Lucky Luciano were the heroes of this time. They depicted a life that was not afforded to most during the depression so being a gangster was heavily emulated. They wore the nicest clothes, they knew the hottest celebrities, and they had the money. With the money, they could pay off the police, government officials, whoever they wanted. But when crime started getting too high, the polarity took effect. The Feds started cracking down on these men, they couldn't pin Alcohol on them so they would pin them with tax evasion and other petty crimes. When these criminals were sentenced to jails like Alcatraz, they were often disconnected from the world of life and leisure. When they were finally released alcohol was legal and their businesses were no longer as profitable. FDR fixed the economy so alcohol wasn't a big thing anymore. Because these criminals were displaced from illusion interruption they went crazy and tended to want to go back to jail.

When the Recession of 1981 occurred, Ronald Reagan ain't do shit. People were living in the street, people were dying from AIDS, and people were selling crack because it was the only way of a steady income. Selling crack was the only to make a fast buck on the streets, if you lived in America during this time, then you were a "hustler." Hustler's like Rich Porter, Fat Cat, Alpo Martinez, AZ, Midget Molley, Geto, Ricky Ross, Supreme and Pappy Mason were seen as heroes of this time. They depicted a life that was not afforded to most during a recession so being a hustler was heavily emulated. They wore the nicest clothes, they knew the hottest celebrities, and they had the money. With the money they could pay off everyone. When crime started getting too high the Feds had to step in. They couldn't pin millions of dollars of a crack empire on them so they used the background of a high-school project dropout against them. When these criminals were sentenced to jails like Sing Sing, they were disconnected from a world of luxury and leisure. When they are finally released crack is no longer cool. Bill Clinton resided over one of the biggest economic expansions in U.S. history so no one wanted to smoke crack as much. Because these criminals were displaced from illusion interruption, they went crazy and tended to want to go back to jail.

"Same old shit, different day."

"Dear Fellas: I can't believe how fast things move on the outside. I saw an automobile once when I was a kid but now they're everywhere. The world went and got itself in a big damn hurry."

People tend to think that a child's fear of the Boogey Man is illogical and will go away with time. Well if it works for Boogey Man, it can work for recession. Don't believe me, watch this

"Tommy, do all your homework or the Boogey man 'll get you!" "No mom not the Boogey Man!" "Yes the Boogey Man so you have to all your homework" "Yes mom, I'll do my homework"

"Americans need to start purchasing American if they don't want a recession!" "No, not a recession!" "Yes a recession so ya'll have to start buying American" "Okay, I'll buy American"

The same fear that is fostered in children is the same fear that is fostered in adults. Ya'll really should have listened to Margaret Kuhn when she was alive. Ah well, long live Gray Panthers!

The recession means nothing without economic prosperity and these economic prosperities mean nothing without recession. Bill Clinton wouldn't be revered as the president who presided over one of the biggest surpluses in U.S history had it not been for Ronald Reagan. Franklin D. Roosevelt would have not founded the New Deal if the Great Depression wouldn't have existed so you should understand you need both. But because you need both, you should understand that both don't exists. If something were actually real, there would be no need to explain it. You wouldn't need a book; you wouldn't need a television you wouldn't need anything that tells you that something is there, because if it's there, it will always be there, regardless of what you learn. You know how people know when they're in love? I don't know, you tell me.

Most people only see in black and white, they can't see grey. They look at recession as all bad, and look at prosperity as all good. They can't look at both and make a decision. But it's not easy when you're surrounded by internet blogs that read:

Top Ten Ways to see that you're in a Recession

If you have no money, you're in a recession

If you have no job, you're in a recession

If you live in the projects, you're in a recession

If you have to check the balance of your account before withdrawing, you're in a recession

If your boyfriend is cheating on you, you're in a recession

If have no toilet paper and have to use the bathroom, you're in a recession

If girls won't come home with you after you them a drink, you're a recession

If you voted for Barack Obama, you're in a recession

If you've ever enjoyed a Happy Meal for the toy and not the food, you're in a recession

Instead of questioning the legitimacy of these assertions, you know what niggas do? "Omg, we're really in a recession! I knew I should I should have brought toilet paper!" These blogs tend to be effective because they apply to everyone, but to make them more effective bloggers focus these general occurrences that happen to everybody and then apply it to a certain demographic. So if they said that "1 in every four people will die because of the recession" they'll be right, because people always die, but because there's speculative cause it'll make people say "Damn there's really a recession!". There is no conspiracy, there's just nature, but people tend to distort natural things with speculation. Illusion interruption.

If 50 stores closed down in Idaho, did it ever occur to you that maybe those stores weren't ever really necessary? Maybe Idaho did just fine with ten. Macy's all over America were going out of business, but the one on 34th Street is still there. CEOs are getting fired from Goldman Sachs, but McDonalds is still hiring. So is this really a recession or is people just crying over spilled milk? While you're looking behind you at the way things used to be, niggas are focusing on the way things are. The CEOs are the ones who get the hardest during every recession. They have stocks and investments, but if that fails they're fucked, period. Those CEOs who received their Master's in Economics can't get a job so easily now. They're too over-qualified for entry level positions. Aside from that, these niggas are just plain old. Poor people will see this and say "Good for those niggas! That's what they get for stealing pension." Rich people suffer just like poor people. They may have money when it's good but when it 360s let's see what happens.

No one is gonna hire a 64 year-old CEO to deliver pizzas on a bike, when they have a perfectly good 17 year-old who won't complain about their legs and won't complain about the $10 an hour they receive because they've never made over $50,000. So they're fine with the entry level, however, Mr. "Willy Loman" is too proud to accept something that is beneath him, so he'll put himself and his family though suffering to save some family legacy that no one cares about. So they won't take a job pays $8.15 an hour because they're used to getting paid $750,000 a year. So when they have to move from that nice house in Long Island to that two bedroom in Flatbush, when they have to give up that M6 for a Honda, when they have to give up that Hi-def for a black-and-white, these same CEOs show you who they are, everyone else. Some of them can't take it and decide to commit suicide. The same things that make you laugh make cry. These CEOs have watched their illusion interruptions be destroyed by a word, so what happens? Displacement, confusion, and insanity.

"I don't say he's a great man. Willie Loman never made a lot of money. His name was never in the paper. He's not the finest character that ever lived. But he's a human being, and a terrible thing is happening to him. So attention must be paid. He's not to be allowed to fall in his grave like an old dog. Attention, attention must finally be paid to such a person."

Because the kids are raised to be like their parents and preserve the family legacy, you know what they do? The same shit. These kids become pressured and forced into a life that has only route. Illusion Interruption.

"I'm gonna show you and everybody else that Willy Loman did not die in vain. He had a good dream. It's the only dream you can have - to come out number-one man. He fought it out here, and this is where I'm gonna win it for him."

"Out with the old in with the new"

This will always be the case, because this is life. The poor in one generation will become rich in the next. The rich generation will become poor in the next. The poor kids in the 70s won't allow their kids to be poor in the 80s. The rich parents in 80s will lose their stock and their kids will grow up poor in the 90s.

Don't get mad at me at me I'm just the messenger. You know what's gonna be funny about this? Educated people are gonna say "You can tell this kid never went to college."

And I'll reply with the only fact I have, this book.

If niggas don't wanna listen to you, why listen to them?

"It's a recession, everybody's broke!"

Well is it still a recession if you've never had money?

And
Is

When you are able to understand what aspects of your life is controlled by illusion interruption, and what aspects is reality intervention you have achieved Freedom Revelation. Freedom Revelation is the ability to negate coercion and necessity. When you are able to achieve Freedom Revelation, you can no longer be controlled by another person's words because you realize that another person's doctrine has the ability to enslave your mind. Freedom Revelation is attainable by struggling with the concepts of illusion interruption and reality intervention. When you are finally able to do this, you can look on things impartially and make sound judgment. Freedom Revelation doesn't shun peoples' opinions. It actually takes each person's opinion into equal consideration, regardless of "race," "age," "intelligence" or "experience."

To illustrate my point, when you watch debates on television you often see one image being pushed. This image, representing the "ideal" person, is always shown. The person dresses "professional," knows "history," speaks "well," and is usually a "male." In addition to this, they also are usually someone of "matured age." Watching this continually, you begin to now believe that the only people capable of "enlightened conversation" are older men who are able to cite historical facts at whim with the help of a vast vocabulary. When you begin to believe this, you are placed within illusion interruption.

Because you are in illusion interruption, the repetition of this image causes you to accept it. So if a child, women, someone who is unable to speak "correctly," or someone who can't cite history well you begin to discount their opinion. Not because you actually want to, but because this is all you've been shown. Even worse, you begin to downplay your own abilities for the sake of illusion interruption. Seeing a physical image inherent in their mental abilities causes you to set yourself in contrast. As a result, you assume that anyone who looks like them is capable of the same things.

"In equating physical beauty with virtue, she stripped her mind, bound it, and collected self-contempt by the heap."

This is how those who understand illusion interruption are able to control reality intervention. All the person has to do is learn the demographic and adapt to its illusion. What this does is allows them to assume the role of an authority figure in order to serve their purpose. Rapists often pretend to be cops, firefighters, lawyers and family friends to have their purpose served. You know Ted Bundy was able to elude the cops for so long? Because he didn't fit the mold of rapists, cops looked at his profile and because he was a college student they said "Not him, must be a mistake." You know how David Berkowitz was able to get away? Cops thought he was too chubby to be a killer; they filed him as a witness. Serial killers are able to maneuver through society because they understand how society works. They expose the faults in society by getting away with the wildest shit. Personally, I wish I knew what a rapists and a killer looked like.

When David Berkowitz shot people he didn't run, he walked. Cops would look for someone who fled from a crime scene; they wouldn't pay attention to someone who casually walked. Because David Berkowitz understood the statistical infrequencies in criminals, he was repeatedly said to be a witness. Ted Bundy knew that of himself he couldn't get females into a car, but he knew cops could. He knew firefighters could, he knew family friends could so he used that to his advantage. Fucked up isn't it.

If a teacher and student were to argue over a topic, who would believe? Most people would side with the teacher because they are taught that teacher's know what they're talking about. Even if the child's right, most students being controlled by illusion interruption will side with the teacher. The students don't believe they're biased, they just believe its **normal**, because they were taught to do so. People are far from ignorant, they're educated.

The only way this illusion can be broken is if the teacher feeds an illusion so extreme that the body is forced to reject it with reality intervention. But, the only reason you were forced to respond with reality interruption is because you were over-exposed to illusion interruption. This is still illusion within itself; because if an illusion interruption had never been introduced, you would have never responded with reality intervention.

Let's do it like this: Adolf Hitler was able to take over Germany by assuming the role of Chancellor and becoming Anti-Semitic. He boasted about the "perfect Aryan race" of Germany, ironically he wasn't German, he was from Austria. When Hitler failed, he committed suicide. Who do you think was at the Nuremberg Trails? Not Hitler! He killed himself. I'll tell you who... "Stupid ass niggas." Illusion interruption. Politicians in the south during segregation wanted to win. They probably didn't like the word "nigger" but they knew "poor white trash" loved to hate "niggers." So the campaign trail in the south became a "Nigger Shouting Match." Whoever said "nigger" the loudest the most wins. So if one politician said "nigger" 47 times and another politician said "nigger" 20 times, who you think won? "Ding, ding, ding, and the winner by unanimous decision by way of "nigger..." This man who said "nigger" for a world record of 47 times in one paragraph! He must hate niggers." Ask a southern citizen who voted for the politician what was his policies, I'd bet you they'd say something like "Well I don't know much about his politics, but one thing's for sure, he hates niggers just like me! He said it 47 times!" Ask this same southerner who's outraged about the passing of the Voting Act of 1964 you'll hear a whole different person "Man that lying cheating conniving politician ain't done nothin' but use niggers as a way to get into office, now my kids gotta school with niggers!" That's too bad, if you would've voted for the politician who said "nigger" 20 times maybe segregation wouldn't have ended. Illusion interruption.

Rappers usually jump onto the biggest trend when they come into the industry. 50 Cent changed the game when people found out he was shot nine times. Then a whole bunch of rappers started bragging about getting shot. It became coherent in the lyrics. Niggas actually started bragging about getting shot. Marketing execs were basically staging ways for their rappers to get shot. So if a rapper was shot outside of their concert, that's 20,000 copies. If a rapper was stabbed in a Pizza Hut, that's another 15,000 units. And please don't let the rapper shoot back! Certified platinum, illusion interruption.

Learn the demographic, adapt to its illusion, become an authority figure. Illusion interruption.

Another concrete example of this allegory would be celebrities. When you are transmitted the image of what a celebrity looks like, you initially are in a state of skepticism. However, if this celebrity is repeatedly shown constantly you begin to like them. But when this celebrity is over-exposed, the body, to equate balance responds with the extreme opposite. Some people find themselves liking Beyonce because they are used to everyone else liking them. So in order to survive, they adapt to liking of Beyonce. But when Beyonce begins to be shown too much, the body takes Beyonce as poison. In order to protect balance, your brain responds with Newton's Third Law of Motion. Now you find yourself not liking Beyonce, but when an explanation is sought after, you are unable to give a reason.

This shows that the body will always give you extremes until you are able to control them. This is why most stars go on hiatus. They know that if they are seen too much they will begin to lose their celebrity status. That's why a lot of celebrities often switch their professions. If a celebrity is able to a lot of things, your unstrained fancy will be stroked. This is why celebrities like Jamie Foxx, Coldplay, Brad Pitt, and Kanye West are such big stars. They often come out for a while then without warning, they go back into hiding. Because you never know what to expect, you end up expecting nothing. This leads to twice the entertainment, because you illusion interruption is not being pushed to an extreme. However stars like Paris Hilton, Lindsay Lohan, and Brittney Spears images are pushed so much we begin to dislike them and not have a logical reason.

Freedom revelation presents the ability for people to look at situations impartially, and choose themselves. Taking into account every opinion, but not valuing any opinion more than the other, reflects the ability to consider reality intervention and illusion interruption but weighing them equally. When you can make choices without permission or coercion from another person, you have achieved freedom revelation.

When looking at these factors, the issue of how this applies to race remains vague to some. To understand race, you must first know the meaning of race. A lot of people say they have a race, but don't know what race means. Race is a local geographic or global human population distinguished as a more or less distinct group by genetically transmitted physical characteristics. Race also pertains to a group of people with a common history, nationality, and geography.

If you study history, you know that life started in Africa. However, due to migration, Africans began to inhabit different areas of the world. When Africans left their original geographical surrounding they had to adapt to other areas of the world. For example, Africans are "dark" because the sun in Africa is hotter than in other places. But when Africans left for Europe and Asia and North America, they began to change. Due to the change of geography, Africans had to adapt to their surroundings. Adaptation means that you are able to conform to a given situation. It is also a hereditary alteration in an organism that facilitates its survival and reproduction.

So when Africans began to inhabit Europe, the sun was not as hot. So what this caused is an adaptation to their surroundings. Some Africans died off because they were unable to change, but the ones who were considered strong survived. That's the idea of Darwinism, only the strong survive. This idea began to become inherent in their culture. So if you couldn't survive in Europe then you were not European. As you know, Europe is way colder than Africa, so the climate forced the pigmentation of Africans to become lighter. After a while, you had someone who looked nothing like an African.

When some Europeans returned back to Africa, their physical appearance shocked Africans because they never seen someone so light. Although they looked different, Africans still accepted them because they're all the same. But when Europeans couldn't stand Africa's sun, couldn't eat the same food, didn't listen to the same music and talked differently, a division in cultures happened.

Looking different didn't define your characteristics; it was the things you did that defined your "race." Because Africans had a physical reality mixed with a mental fancy, Africans became consumed by illusion interruption. So in order to preserve the African "race," Africans exiled Europeans. The animals that were in Africa weren't in Europe so Europeans ate differently. Because their experiences were different, their language was as well. To understand more, more has to be explained.

Culture is defined by the totality of socially transmitted behavior patterns, acts, beliefs, institutions and other products of human work and thought. Culture is also the predomination attitudes and behavior that characterizes a group or organization. Culture breeds, it is a development of the intellect through training or education. One of the many concepts that contribute to culture is artistic activities, such as literature, art and music. An art is the human effort to imitate, supplement, alter or counteract the work of nature. That is why art is significant to a culture, because it captures the illusion of the race. Ironically, although art is made to define a culture, it always ends up uniting other races through influence and inspiration.

Culture is based on present situations. So culture would be defined as reality intervention. It becomes illusion interruption when it is passed down. Tradition is the passing down of culture from generation to generation, especially by oral communications. Tradition then becomes a set customs viewed as a coherent body of precedents influencing the present. When you are taught your culture, you are in illusion interruption because you are bred to be like your ancestors. If you understand the past, you can control the present. That is the purpose of child rearing.

Language is significant to different cultures because it reflects their understanding of the world. If you're able to use a language and understand it, you would be considered to be apart of a culture. If all you spoke was Japanese, regardless of your physical appearance, you would be considered Japanese because that's the only culture you understand. When a language is completely understood, slang is born. Slang is playful and commonly reflects your present mind state. It is deliberately used in place of standard terms for excitement, humor and irreverence.

Slang is commonly considered disrespectful because it doesn't hold the original language to its highest regard. Language would be illusion interruption whereas slang would be reality intervention. Slang takes the "mother" language and ridicules it. It is done by taking something that has one meaning and using the same the word for another situation, homonym if you will. If you didn't understand slang you would assume that "cat" meant the animal, but when "cat" is used as a slang term it is now a common person.

People who hold history in high regard often despise slang because they feel that slang displays ignorance. Ironically, people who use slang laugh at the people who are unable to understand it because it displays their own ignorance. The relationship of language and slang is seen in Newton's Third Law of Motion. For example, children are raised to use "proper language" in society. Children usually have no problem with this, but when "proper language" is emphasized too much it causes the body and the mind to reject "proper language" with an extreme opposite. This extreme opposite becomes slang. To ridicule "proper language," slang takes all of the words from the "mother language" and uses it for things that they experience personally.

Slang is a form of satire because it pokes fun at a personal flaw to expose another persons'. Teenagers are often called stupid by adults for using slang. Ironically, adults don't understand the present situation in which slang is used because they're focused on the past. So teenagers only end up laughing at adults. The same ignorance that teenagers are accused of when it comes to understanding language is the same ignorance that adults display when they can't understand slang.

It is important to understand that although slang is reality intervention, it is still a form of illusion interruption because if there was no past language then there would be no present slang. When you are able to see that language and slang are equally important, you can understand everyone putting you in Freedom Revelation. Slang reflects intelligence because you have to understand all the concepts of language to make slang significant. If you don't understand language, you can't make slang.

Slang is illusion interruption because when teenagers grow up they hold on to their slang and teach it to their kids. Their kids, being taught the language of their parents, begin to rebuke it and make slang from their parents' language. When someone's able to look at the relationship of slang and language and see that they are equally productive, they now become able to make their own language. When you are able to make your own language, you are now able to make your own culture, when you are able to make your own culture, you can make your own race.

The Tower of Babel is an exceptional paradigm for the relationship between language and slang. In the book of Genesis, the Tower of Babel was built to reach the heavens. According to the biblical account, everyone in Babylon spoke one united language. Nimrod, the king of Babylon, built this tower to commemorate his rule. According to the Bible's doctrine, because it reflected the glory of man and not the glory of God, God scrambled the languages of the people who built it causing miscommunication. The differences in languages ultimately led to the discontinuation of the Tower.

Due to the Bible's effectiveness in dogmatism, this story is often understood literally. People literally built a Tower to reach the heavens, and God in order to preserve his kingdom, scrambles the language? This story is true, but specific details of this are often distorted for control. When you are raised with the bible, you aren't allowed to grasp an individual understanding. The bible is often taught one way so that it holds control. People are usually forced to see things that aren't really there. But in order to preserve livelihood, people will just conform to whatever the establishment says. That's how religion starts.

Nimrod, the king of Babylon, was portrayed as a hunter in the bible. This remains to be seen in the dictionary, Nimrod means hunter. But because he was the ultimate cause for the division in language, Nimrod also means silly, foolish, or stupid. So although he was originally a king, because he divided his people, he became stupid. If you were to say Nimrod during his reign you would be making a connotation to the King of Babylon or a hunter. After the Tower of Babel, if you said nimrod you were calling someone stupid. The people who were around during the reign of Nimrod may hear their child say "My friends a nimrod!" and assume that the child's friend is a hunter or a king. But the child is calling their friend stupid. So when the parent meets their child's friend they'll say, "So my child says you're a hunter." The friend, being confused by the statement, will say, "Huh?" The parent will say "Aren't you a nimrod?" The child having their own understanding of the word nimrod will reply, "Yes." This will force the parent to say, "So that must mean you're a hunter, correct?" The friend, still confused, will say "No." The parent, now becoming frustrated, will say "If you're a Nimrod, then you're a hunter." The child will disagree saying that, "Nimrod means stupid." The parent, unable to understand the logic of the child, will probably end up forcing their child to avoid the friend. But not before saying, "I don't understand your generation, something is wrong with the world today." Tower of Babel.

That is the reason why all words do not have one precise meaning. Throughout time the word will always change, based on the present situation. But the present situation is only more significant if you are forced to understand the past. The only reason atheism exists is because they were forced to believe in God. If the belief in God had not been emphasized then the birth of atheism would have not occurred. Because kids were over-exposed to God, their body began to reject the idea of God. The extreme action of religion leads to the opposite extreme of atheism. Atheism is a religion within itself. Atheism, like religion, is illusion interruption. Atheists say "Oh my God!" the same way Christians do.

"No one is so thoroughly superstitious as the godless man."

Anyone willing to accept a race is racist. Anyone willing to accept a sex is sexist. Anyone willing to accept sexual preference is a homophobe. If you identify yourself with a race, you are basically exhibiting the belief that because of your physical characteristics you have an intrinsic capability that is unattainable in other races. If you identify yourself with a sex, you are now stating that because you are a "male" and have a "penis" you are capable of achieving things that is unattainable to women. If you say you're a heterosexual, you are saying that because you like the "opposite sex" you are "normal." All of these beliefs are illusion interruption.

But don't get it twisted! It works the other way as well. Homosexuals are pushed to an extreme; ironically they have done some discriminating on heterosexuals as well. For example, if you're not a "homo" you can't say "faggot," because it's a slur, but it is quite alright for a "homo" to say it. Sounds familiar?

Females won't allow a heterosexual man to see them naked but it's quite alright for a homosexual to see them naked. Wait isn't that discrimination? Females don't see it this way, they only see illusion interruption. So sometimes boys will act "gay" to see girls naked and feel on them without being called perverts. You may say these boys are psychopaths but the real psychopath is the homophobic sexist.

Boys see girls as "devious and sneaky." Some males believe that all women "ain't shit" and all deserve to be treated like objects. Because it is the social construct that makes this **nirmal**, this open disrespect towards women as cool. So this whole culture reflects this view of "how to keep your girl in check." If a man cheats he's a pimp, if female cheats she's a "ho," "harlot," "whore," "skeezer," "smut" or foul. The reason why females are "devious" and "sneaky" is because society makes it okay for males to violate women but not okay the other way around.

So a female couldn't openly brag about having sex promiscuously because she's a whore. If there were no pressures on females like there is on males, females would be just as loose. However because society often praises one and not the other, females are seen as dangerous and deceitful. This is illusion interruption; men constantly deceive girls because that's what being a "man" is all about. So it's only fair that female's fake orgasms, give fake numbers, don't answer their phones, and tell boys that they have big penises when they know it's not true. Fair is Fair, I guess.

Feminists, although heavily oppressed throughout history, seem to have this superior attitude that females are better. Although some feminists have seen first handedly what the patriarch system does to women, some feminist still insist on female hegemony. What Freud defines as "penis envy" I define as illusion interruption. Ironic, isn't it?

Have you been in a relationship where your "gender role" destroyed your life? (I sound like a talk show) You may like someone but because society tells you how to behave, you know have to accommodate and adapt. So instead of telling someone plain out "I like you, let's go out." Your friends will force you to some cliché line that they found in a "How to" (by a psychologists who ironically has problems catching himself) book on picking up girls. Now although you may have a good chance with this girl, saying something stupid flushes your chances. And then the same friends that told you to do it laugh at you.

Females are often targeted when they are by themselves. Not because all men are predators, but more because when females are with friends it tends to be a group decision instead of an individual one. So if a boy approaches a female, the "clan" then swarms the dude and wards him off. So often bad relationships aren't even due solely to the couple, but more because of the couples' friends. You know exactly what I'm talking about? He said, she said.

The racism that was accused of MTV in the 80s is the same racism that is displayed on BET. In the 80s, it took a while for MTV to play Michael Jackson. Now it'll take a while for BET to play Fall Out Boy. "Separate but Equal." That was established in 1869; 140 years later it's still the same... Illusion interruption. If everything is equal, why separate it?

OJ was acquitted on the charges of killing Nichole Simpson; the police who beat up Rodney King were acquitted. Separate but Equal, better yet, illusion interruption.

How do you know of your race, your sex or your sexual preference? Do you grow up just getting epiphanies, or are you taught? (Gender roles, self-identity, ethnicity awareness, etc) So the beliefs that many people stand by is a control set by illusion interruption. If a seven-year-old boy wants an Easy Bake Oven, he's "gay." If a little girl wants to play football, she's a "dike." If a boy dresses too fashionable he's a "fag," if a girl likes to wear basketball shorts she's an "Ag." If a man wants to be a stay-at-home dad, he's not a real man. If a woman wants to obtain an executive position, she's laughed at. If a "black" person uses "big words," they're trying to be "white." If a "white girl" wants to be a rapper, she's told to be an accountant. Thank God for gender roles, self-identities and ethnical awareness!

That is the reason why Prince and the Revolution were the biggest stars in the 80s. When "Purple Rain" came out, their appearance was so unusual. Their androgynous appearance was so intriguing and fascinating that it started this big movement where boys were looking like girls and girls looked like boys. Androgyny, which means not having a specified gender trait, became the culture of Pop music in the 80s. Although Prince looked virtually like a woman, he was able to attract some of the baddest females in the business. Females were wearing pants, men were wearing heels. Females were cutting their hair; men were getting Perms and Jheri Curls. "Pretty Boys" would get all the girls (and sometimes attract men) because it was hard to tell the difference. Sometimes "Pretty Boys" are so "pretty" that they tend to repulse females. Some girls find themselves thinking, "He's too pretty to like girls." Androgyny is illusion interruption.

Androgynous names like Stacy, Dorian, Sean, Tyler, Ashley, Chris, Marion, and Marlon confuse people because they're all illusion interruptions. These names are already prescribed to certain genders, so when we hear a certain name we start to think about what we are familiar with. Like Stacy is generally a female name. But if a boy is named Stacy then the illusion is distorted with reality intervention.

I've even caught myself baffled when I met a girl who was named Dion. There were times when she would call my house and my friends would answer the phone and say "Hello?" and she'd say "Is Yahdon there?" and my friends would ask, "Who's this?" and she'd say "Dion."

They would get me and ask "Yo! I didn't know you like boys." And at first I was confused at the statement. So I asked "What?" and they'd reply "A *dude* named Dion called." And I would think like Dion is an asexual name. But my friends wanted to be funny so what they would make jokes of saying how I liked boys. At first, I would get mad and for a while I would call her by her middle name because it was more *feminine* than Dion. Then I realized that people make jokes regardless, it's a part of life. One thing for sure, when they finally seen Dion, those jokes stopped.

It's understandable why people are homosexuals and "sell-outs." There's no room for personal freedom in social constructs. But only the oppressed will accept being oppressed. Regardless of what you do, someone is always gonna say something "negative." So think about it this way, Recognition reflects accomplishment and criticisms are the best compliments. If you're not being talked about, then you don't exist. Only fantasies remain secrets because realities are always exposed. So the more someone says the bigger your existence, if no one says anything then you become another Biggie song "You're Nobody Til' Somebody Kills You."

Everything you do will always be scrutinized because that's how people are. Someone will always give you a label; the label only becomes true when you accept it yourself. "Gay" people aren't really "gay." It's just that people are scrutinized for everything they do, that they say to themselves, "Fuck it, no matter what I do imma be called gay, so I guess I'm gay." So what happens now is the person becomes "gay" to prove a point. In reality, they haven't proved anything because it was already assumed that the person was gay. So now the person who points the finger becomes right. Self-fulfilling prophecy.

But what this does also is make "gays" discriminate against "straights." So if a straight man were a model, there would be an assumption that they're gay, because they model. Regardless of what they like, they're gay to the industry because apparently only "homos" model.

"Nigger" is the same way. "Black people" were called "nigger" for everything they did for so long they said "Fuck it, no matter what I do imma be called nigger, so I guess imma nigger." So they took this word and prescribed it to themselves and everyone that looks like them. So if you're not the physical archetype of "what nigger a looks like," then you're not a "real nigger." You know, "real niggers" don't go to school, they play ball, they go to jail, they leave their kids, and they do time for other people's crime. "Because these are real niggers!"

So I'm guessing Larry Bird, Pete Maravich, Rick Barry and Jerry West are "real niggers" because they play ball. Albert Einstein, Pablo Picasso, Vincent Van Gogh, Ludwig Wittgenstein are "real niggers" because they hated school. Charles Manson, Al Capone, and David Berkowitz are "real niggers" because they went to jail. Dick Cheney, Oliver North, and John Edgar Hoover are "real niggers" because they don't snitch. And Thomas Jefferson must be the "realest nigger" because he had mad kids and didn't take care of a lot of them. Can you say "Real Nigga!?!"

But niggas won't see it this way. They'll see illusion interruption. They'll see Michael Jordan, Julius Erving, Lebron James, Wilt Chamberlain as the only "real niggas" that play ball because they can dunk. "You know white boys can't jump, just ask Brent Barry!" "Yeah Albert Einstein and Pablo Picasso are cool but real niggas are niggers like Huey P. Newton and Martin Luther King Jr." The man who made that phenomenal speech on the steps of the Lincoln Memorial has a doctorate. And so does the "real nigger" who co-founded the Black Panthers, Just call Martin and Huey "Dr. Niggers." Frank Lucas, Alpo Martinez and Nicky Barnes snitched. You still know what a *real nigger* look like? Because I can see a real racist.

"Black people" often take offense to the word "nigger," but will openly and readily accept "black," "colored," and "African-American." The logic most "black people" exhibit when asked why nigger is "offensive" is "Because it was a term used by the "white man" to control slaves." Well if that's true, then what about "black?" You need opposition to exist. In order to have a hero you need a villain. The only way slave masters could makes slaves believe that they were "white" is if they told slaves that they were "black." When most slave masters described their slaves they were "black niggers" not just niggers, because niggers aren't only black. Look at the context "*black* nigger," that *should* insinuate that niggers aren't only "black" because if that were true nigger would be an adjective, not a noun. Nigger can be used as an adjective on some occasions, but so can "white." You know that white trash nigger that everydang? And it really be white.

Black is not an African word, it's an English word just like "nigger." So if "nigger" is offensive, then "black" should be too. A lot of "black people" don't believe that they're "niggers," but will believe that they're black. Black is the color of this ink. If you can look in the crayon box, grab a black crayon and show me someone who is the same color as the crayon, so much so that the crayon and the person's skin complexion is ambiguous to each other, I'll shut up right now. Most people will read this and say, "Well that's a bad example, because everyone knows that black is also used for a skin color." And I will reply with the Tower of Babel, complete and utter satire. I see why niggas don't take niggas seriously.

The reason why "black people" take offense to the word "nigger" is because they're just as racist as the "white" people they accuse. Any word sets a racist off. Like if a "white man" said "Why are you always late?" And the racist says "Watchu tryna say about black people? You think all black people are late?" The employer never made any connotation towards the employees' race, but the employee did.

This is common for the "average black activist" who prides themselves on taking personal problems and blaming it on their race and the subjugation of the "dreaded white-man." because they know that "white people" fret from racial tension due to American history. Everything that happens is "Because they're black" or "Because this is a white' mans country." "I partied last night and drunk too much, fuck it I'm not going to work today!" Then when they get fired, "It's because they're black." Really? That party had nothing to do with it? Guess you really are a nigger; better yet maybe you're just racist.

Words are just words, period. It's not until you use the word within a certain connotation or context does the word gain meaning. For example, you can say to your friends "car" and they'll be like "What?" It's not completely understood until you place a connotation or a context around it. That's what makes a sentence, a complete thought. So if you were to say "I'm going to go buy a car." They will now understand your purpose for saying "car."

Take the word "brother" for example. During the Black Panther era, brother was used to empower and also became an identifying connotation towards the black race. The reason why the use of "brother" and "sister" were so popular in the 60's and the 70's was for two reasons. First reason, to counteract the self-destructive psyche of the "nigger" who plays Joseph McCarthy and accuses everyone of being racist and they is the real racist. And because the belief that everyone who is black has a shared ancestry of being slaves and being from the motherland which is Africa. So when you said "brotha" or "sista" to someone in the 60s and the 70s you were talking about "blacks."

Because the Black Panther movement was so powerful, everyone wanted be called "brotha" and "sistah" because the Panthers made it cool. But, here comes the racism again. "You can't say brotha, because you ain't black, honky!" So "honkies" began to say "brotha" as a disparaging term for blacks. If a cop said "You seen any brothas run this way?!?" It was already understood that a "brotha" was a black man.

This word was one of power and one of destruction. It was a term used like separate but equal, you know, "blacks only." So it was used only for "blacks" as being cool, but when a "honky" said it, it was no longer cool. So when the word backfired to where everybody thought that all black people were related because they referred to "their own" as "brotha" or "sista" the word showed "black people" just how racist they really are. Although Huey P. Newton made it explicitly direct that he defamed "Black Nationalism" because it promoted the same racism that America was accused of. "Brothas" still saw fit to act like niggers or maybe racists, you choose. Huey was more concerned with helping anyone who needed it.

Today, brotha is used for *every race* as endearment. Think about why.

When looking at words "black people" like **ALL** people, don't look at a word by itself. They are taught what words mean. So it's the parents' job to make sure that the child understands the word. So when we are taught words, the most common way we use it is the same way are parents use it. Now that the context has been defined for us, we go around using the word regularly because it's what we've been taught to do. When the given word doesn't match the current situation it then confuses us. Unable to understand, we go back to our parents. Although it is parents who teach us things, they are not to blame for misguidance. They are basically defining the world for you, the way the world has been defined for them. They give you the world the way they understand it, but we are not our parents, so we have to understand the world for ourselves.

The word ghetto originated in Venice regarding the areas where Jews were forced to live. Today people pride themselves on being from the ghetto, because struggle is the new success. If ghetto could change from a negative so can nigger, couldn't it?

And you won't believe what Neo-Nazi's refer to each other as.

"Brother"

I'll
r

Most kids won't look at it this way due to the division set between a child and an adult. Children are usually considered "invisible" in the eyes of adults. "Be seen not heard." The reason is because adults talk differently around children as oppose to other adults. An adult's assumption of a child's inability to understand them becomes a self-fulfilling prophecy. What the adult will now do is set up a separate language in which one language is used for the child, and a completely different language is used for the adult. Unable to understand the adult language, the child will naturally adapt to the child language. Over time the child begins to study adults. The child begins to see that the same things are defined differently for them as oppose for adults. The child may display their understanding of the "adult" language, but if they are persecuted for this, in order to sustain life a child will now adapt and no longer show its intelligence in reverence towards the adult language.

Instead, what the child will now do is begin to envy the adult language. In addition to the envy, the child will also distrust it as well. Although the child has a phenomenal understanding of the adult language, they know that they can't use it. So as a form of satire, the child will learn to love the child language. Moreover, the child will begin to change the words originally given by the adult for other things. This will now display the adults' stupidity for underestimating the child. The child will now become defined as whatever the adult wants. The adult doesn't see the satire because they are controlled by illusion interruption. Ironically, the child doesn't see the satire either. Although they are currently in reality intervention, they are ultimately controlled also by illusion interruption.

Let's apply this example to slavery. Now most "Africans" were not allowed to read or write. The reason? Because it would distort the illusion that slaves couldn't understand masters. Initially, the slaves that wanted to prove something showed that they understood English and could read as well as write. Because the masters were consumed by illusion interruption it threatened the balance of slavery. So what the masters did was persecute the slaves who could read, write and understand the "adult" language which would be English in this case. The "child" language would be "slave" vernacular, you know "yessuh, I's a good nigga, massa, etc." But because slaves were openly persecuted for breaking illusion interruption, the other slaves adapted and evolved into reality intervention.

This reality intervention entailed that they no longer show reverence towards the English language. All living things would do anything to preserve life. Slaves now knew that they can be killed for learning the adult language, so they no longer *openly* showed that they understood it. Instead, they *openly* showed the reverence for the "child" language. This made the master believe they could control their "slaves." But the whole time the slaves were thinking "You know for a "master," he's a dumb nigger!" Who's really the nigger?

Realistically, anyone who showed someone they could read during this time was the "dumb" slave. You just seen someone get lynched for reading, so why would you show the same person who you've just seen kill someone and say "Look boss, I can read! I'm not a dumb nigger like the others, I's smart." "Sure you are boy, now go get that noose and go hang yourself." Illusion interruption.

Most recent example, There are two ways to talk in society. There's the formal way and the informal way. Formal behavior entails that you refrain from using adverbs and contractions, you address everyone as their surname and you must keep eye-contact. You must know you're subject-verb agreements, your reflexive pronouns, your comma splices and etc. No "racially-charged" jokes, no endearing terms and it is imperative that you be the biggest kiss-ass and brown noser there is. So there becomes a divide in acceptable and unacceptable language.

Before getting a "good" job, people often study "professional" etiquette. They study it so well, they become it. Because there is a standard status of what "professionalism" is, it makes it easier to emulate. An amateur doesn't get paid for what they do but a professional does. So let's watch a professional at work, shall we:

Let's use a typical "black name" for this example... umm oh I got it; Natasha Johnson is perfect (Although Natasha is an Italian name and Johnson is a Hebrew name). Natasha didn't graduate high school and she wants a job as a receptionist for a wealthy Fortune 500 company. She doesn't have a degree but she has a television. Natasha watches television constantly, but because she wants this job bad she'll do anything to get it. She never grew up in a wealthy neighborhood and never attended college so how will she get it?

Natasha begins to watch CNN, NBC, and CBS. She also reads the New York Times, and the Wall Street Journal to become more "acquainted" with the "professional" atmosphere. "Earrings no bigger than nickels, hair can't be too pretentious or ostentatious, clothes and shoes can't attract too much attention but just enough to get the employer to like me and slang has to be thrown out the window for the new slang; 'professional language.'"

Soon Natasha is no longer the college dropout from the projects. She is now Ms. Johnson, a street savvy receptionist who happens to have a vast understanding of the economy and politics. She no longer says "Yo!" she says "Excuse me!" she no longer says "Bitch" she now says "female." She refrains from using the word "nigga" because that is a "bad word," she no longer eats at McDonalds, she eats at Morton's Steakhouse. In a few weeks, Natasha feels confident to go in for that interview at that Fortune 500 Company.

When she goes in she keeps her head high, she flashes that perfect smile, she keeps that eye-contact, firm handshake (even as a "woman") and she remembers everyone's name, and at times she's able to use economic and political references as allegories for her explanations. "Natasha Johnson, you're the perfect candidate for the receptionist position, you start on Monday!" Willy Loman said to Biff "It's not what you know, it's who you know." The media tells Natasha oops... I mean Ms. Johnson that it's "What you know that gets you to who you'll know."

This amateur with the help of the media now has a professional job that pays handsomely. And it's all because of freedom revelation! Ms. Johnson still hangs out on the weekend substituting her signature "female" back to "bitch" when she's with her friends. "Yo bitch! Those rich niggas be payin' bread in Manhattan!" But when Monday morning comes she switches back to Ms. Johnson. What was that Holden? You call her a "phony," Na she's not a "phony." What was that Huck? She's "sivilized" Na she's not "sivilized" She's a professional!

"I'm always saying "Glad to've met you" to somebody I'm not at *all* glad I met. If you want to stay alive, you have to say that stuff, though."

You know the funny thing about money? It seems to be the only sustaining factor that shows us we're all the same. Watch Trading Places if you think I'm lying.

(Still think I'm lying! The New Deal and the Five-Year Plans, look it up.)

"The lack of money is the root of all evil."

Now, let's look at the "African-American's" favorite excuses for the reason why "whites" can't use the word "nigger." Slavery, being the number one reason, is why "white" people can't say "nigger." Racism is another reason why the "white man" can't say "nigger." Lynching is one more reason that the "white man" can't say nigger. Ummm....Rosa Parks is another reason. The assassination of Malcolm X, Martin Luther King Jr, and Huey P. Newton, more reasons. The "distribution" of "AIDS" and "crack" are more reasons. Wait there's more! The unsolved deaths of Tupac Shakur **and** Biggie Smalls are two more reasons. The attempt to impeach Bill Clinton is another reason, followed by 8 years of Bush. And my personal favorite, the New York's Post article of portraying Barack Obama as a monkey. What you have here is the reasons why "white people" can't say "nigger." What you also have is the history of what it means to be "African-American." Wait! How could I forget the most obvious answer? "Because they're not black." Ask this same "black person" if they're racist, they'll sincerely say... "No"

If a "black person" says "nigga" to another "black person" it's ***nigmal***. Let a "white person" say the same word, under the same connotation. Regardless of context this "white person" is automatically racist, and told not to say that word because "they're not black". So of course this "white person" will naturally think that niggas are black, because they've been told, "Only blacks can say it." Still don't see any racism?

Although no one in present day America experienced the African Slave Trade, people will beat you with it to the point that you want to lynch them. If you were to ask a "proud black man" about slavery you will be taken on this long journey to where Africans were this "perfect" race who never did any wrong to anybody. Then, the "barbaric white man" comes and starts capturing them by the millions. Being crammed on boats, where Africans had to defecate and urinate on each other, Africans were made to live there for 6 months. Finally making it over to the Americas, they were beaten, forced to take a different name and sold in auctions. The "slave-master" then began to kill all of the "smart" slaves and leave the "dumb" ones alone. In addition, white men raped their slaves breeding "Light-Skinned Uncle Tom Sell-Outs" (You know like Malcolm and Huey who were both light-skinned) who told on the runaways and got them caught. Slavery, from the perspective of a "proud black man."

Ask this same "black man" if they've ever read Uncle Tom's Cabin, they'll tell you "No, that book is racist!" Ask them who Harriet Beecher Stowe is, and they'll say some real nigga shit… "Who?" I know niggas is reading this right now and saying, "This nigga setting black people back." (If that were possible, BET, Jesse Jackson and Al Sharpton did it a while ago.) "This nigga a sell-out." I'll let you tell it "proud black activist."

I betchu Abraham Lincoln knows who Harriet Beecher Stowe is. "The little lady who started the big war." "What war is this nigga talking about?"

Jay-Z said one time "don't make me get the dude with the afro." Go get him, because he teaches at Princeton, not Howard. And I'm the sell-out? Hmm "You can't lead the people if you don't love the people. You can't save the people, if you don't serve the people." Barry White said "Practice what you Preach" I think now would be the best time. "Racist ass niggas." Smh. The only people who can make a difference are the people who see no difference. Think about that "Black Existentialist."

My question is, is slavery a mind state or a physical boundary? When hearing the word slavery, most people automatically prescribe it to "black people." In addition, the images of whelps, lynchings, chains and shackles, and the pictures of forty slaves outside of "Massas'" house come to mind because that's what you've been taught by slavery. Ask anybody if they're a slave, they think about the most understood context of the word and then think about the African slave trade. So when they take this word into consideration, they say to themselves "Well I'm not in chain and shackles, and I'm not being beat or hung from a tree," so they'll answer "No."

A slave is a person bound in servitude as the property of a person or household. One who is abjectly subservient to a specified person or influence would also be considered a slave. Ironically, the word slave now means to be worked beyond logic. "Yo, these niggas be slaving me, they must think its still 1775 or something." Ever heard it, quite sure you have. People being taught what slavery was now believe that because the specific examples aren't pertinent now, they can't possibly be a slave. This mind state shows the control of illusion interruption. "Black people" are controlled by the past, so they remain in illusion interruption. Even if some of them are in reality intervention, they are only there because the past was emphasized too much. It's not until "black people" are able to look at both the past and present evenly do the understand freedom revelation.

Because the African slave trade is the most common understood meaning of a slave, a "white man" could **never** call a "black man" a slave. Ironically, the "proud black man" will accept being called "black" by the same "white man."

"This is God's curse on slavery!—a bitter, bitter, most accursed thing!—a curse to the master and a curse to the slave! I was a fool to think I could make anything good out of such a deadly evil."

If you want to understand the history of the "black man" then you must know the history of everyone else. You cannot look at any struggle that "black people" have made without crediting another "race." Because that within itself is racism, not "reverse" racism just plain racism.

A "black person" will proudly boast about the Black Panthers, Martin Luther King Jr, Marcus Garvey, and Black Power. Ask them about John Brown, Susan B. Anthony, Harriet Beecher Stowe, Mark Twain and Bob Dylan and you'll hear "Fuck outta here, they're not black!"

In the 1936 Hitler bragged about being Aryan and the superiority of the German race. Ask Hitler about Jesse Owens and you'll hear "Ficken Sie aus hier, ist er nicht deutsch" See what I mean?

The Silk Road was one of the most prosperous trade routes in the history of mankind. The Silk Road was a figurative name for its actual purpose. Like the saying "Silky smooth," the Silk Road worked smoothly in bringing integration to different cultures. Asia, Europe and Northern Africa were once competitors, now because of the Silk Road they became allies. These countries realized that, divide and conquer, although a strong tactic, would not work in a changing environment. During the time of the Silk Road, cultural awareness boosted immensely. In addition, because Europeans, Africans, and Asians were so used to being divided and conquered by their "own people," they began to despise their "own people."

Being told to stay within their "own race" and avoid all other races forced the extreme opposite. The children of the kings and queens of Europe, Asia, and Africa were exposed to one image of beauty that they began to reject it. The kings and queens of these countries were people who represented the idea of what it meant to be a part of Africa, Europe, and Asia. The kings and queens replicated the past. So much so, it instilled fear within all those who didn't believe in history.

History is a narrative of events; a story basically. It is a chronological record of events which shows the development of a people. History gives explanations on phenomenon and marvels of the past generations to promote awareness within the enduring generations. If a child understands their "history" then they can control their present. If they can control their present then they can influence the future. Ironically the same way they're able to control is the same way their able to be controlled, because they rule the world through the minds of illusion interruption.

That's why it's so important that royalty know their "history." History, illusion interruption 101, became the foreground on judging royalty. Everything became based on how the "ancestors" did it. The elders held arbitrary competitions in which they gave children situations that the elders already knew the answer to. When the children gave answers to the elders they were then asked of their method. If a child used the same method as the elder then they were openly rewarded with praise. If a child got it wrong and used the same method, they were scolded and told to do it again. Now, if a child got the same answer and didn't use the same method then something happened.

The elders would ask the child, "Who taught you that?" The child will say, "I taught myself." Unable to understand the logic behind the statement, the elders will begin to fear the child. Although the elders fear the child, they will not show it. Instead, the elders will no longer pay attention to the child who understands it the way they do, they will now worship the child who understands the same things differently.

The elders will ask the child to show how they got to their answer. The child will naturally listen and show them. What you have now is an illusion interruption shifted on its axis. The original illusion interruption was the rule of the elders, but now you see that the elders worship the child. The elders and the child know this, but society could never know because that will destroy the illusion. Children don't care about credit, but the elders do, so the elders can take something learned by the child in secret and openly teach it. This now keeps illusion interruption on its original path.

The problem arises when the child who taught the elders of their knowledge is now mocked by their peers. So if the child were to say, "That was my idea." Because the children don't understand the logic of the statement, they will laugh. Moreover, they will begin to tease the child for being foolish and stupid. The child, becoming furious, now goes to the elders and pleads with the elders to tell their friends that the idea was his. The elders, not wanting to disrupt illusion interruption, deny the claim that they learned anything from a child. Even more so, the elders begin to use the illusion interruption to their advantage. The elder will say something like "You think a "child" taught me something?"

Because most people are stuck in the illusion interruption that only elders teach and children learn, they will side with the elder. The child, confused by everyone's stupidity, is now called crazy and put away. While the child is confined, they become bitter with elders, children, and society altogether. So the child becomes a rebel in order to get their revenge. Once this child becomes a rebel, they become illusion interruption.

The elders, being conflicted with their own illusion interruption, decide to secretly outlaw individualism. Another trail is given to the children. Whoever gets the answer "correct" is now deemed "royalty." Whoever gets it "wrong" is deemed "peasants." Whoever gets the answer "correct" answer but uses the "wrong" method is killed. What the elders have now done is used freedom revelation as a means to strengthen their illusion interruption. So history has now defaulted itself. "It's not what you know; it's what you can prove."

(Hitler took the word Aryan that once applied to Indo-Iranians and switched it to reflecting the perfect German; you know the stereotype "blonde hair, blues eyes." Hitler also took the swastika that was an iconic symbol for Germany from the Hindu religion which originally meant "good luck," now it is a symbol that evokes fear because of its most recent "education." Because of education someone could never name their child Adolf. Even though Adolf was a name before Hitler, he basically ruined it for any kids whose name is Adolf, because all of these kids will have to be subject to hear "You killed Jews.") Too bad I can't prove it, ah well.

So the kings and queens are made to resemble the past in every way. They have to eat what the ancestors eat, they have to listen to the same music, and they have to wear the same clothes, they have to be more than like the ancestors, they **have to be** the ancestors. What this does is keep illusion interruption on its axis. It keeps the control within the elders and it keeps the children controlled. This culture, this history, this tradition has become a heritage. This heritage has now become a dynasty. In a matter of years, this dynasty will become an empire. This empire begins to grow like a fungus on your consciousness into something greater, this dynasty now becomes a nation. This nation, through "brutality" "violence" and "fear" becomes a country. And because everyone finally understands the same illusion interruption, this country becomes a continent. When people begin to "die" for the "establishment," the continent becomes the world. "Ignorance is Bliss"

The "child", being rebuked by society, begins to rebuke themselves to sustain living. The "child" understands that they cannot beat a system that is constructed one way, so they adapt to the given situation of being crazy. As long as the "child" is believed to be crazy, the child won't be killed. The "child" will be "spared" at the expense of the "greater good." The "child" leaves and begins to create a new system. This system is the exact opposite of the original establishment. Although the child believes that they're a revolutionary, they're really a rebel stuck in illusion interruption. The only reason why the child's system is so effective is because they have seen the flaws in the system they hate. If they were never shown a flaw, then they would've never rebuked society, so they're the same. If anything, the child would have to realize that they should be ultimately grateful to the elders who denied them. The child doesn't see it this way, they only see illusion interruption. "Eye for an Eye."

Ironically the child builds a "different" system the same way, but because they are consumed with illusion interruption they don't know this. So they begin to kill those who think differently, praise those who think alike, and scorn those who don't think at all. Through years of constant brutality, violence and fear, you now have an identical system that can "compete" with the original. "Big brother versus little brother, Cain versus Abel."

"What happens when an irresistible force meets an immovable object?" Nothing… Because the child has the same "system" as the elder, nothing happens. They fight, they make peace, they divide themselves, they conquer each other, they fight, they make peace, they divide themselves, they conquer each other, they fight, they make peace, they divide themselves, they conquer each other………………

The same annoyance you feel with reading the same shit is the same annoyance I get with writing the same shit. But what you should realize is that nothing happens. "Why so serious Son?"

So, the Silk Road bred a new love of cultural integration. Because the princes and princesses were forced to embrace history, they rebuked it. They didn't openly show this, because that would destroy the illusion. In addition, they would've been killed. As stated earlier, all living things have the primary concern of sustaining life. So they adapted to the illusion, but didn't evolve into it. They exhibited the illusion of racial-pride and nationalism when they were amongst the "wolves," but when they were amongst the "sheep" they exhibited something different. These princes and princesses were displaying freedom revelation. Like the "love-affair" between Mark Antony and Cleopatra, or the "tragic" love story of Romeo and Juliet, they were forced to accept people because of their history. However, if someone displayed a negative characteristic within their own "culture," the "negative" characteristic was prescribed to the opposing family.

In terms of prescribing negative characteristics to opposing families, I got a few… Oh, "white people" are crazy. "Black people" are violent. "Asians" are docile. If you have a two bedroom apartment and eight people are living in the kitchen, you're "Hispanic." So if you saw a "black person" fighting on the train, they would be a "nigger." If you saw a white man doing the same thing they'll be *acting* like a "nigger." See the confusion.

"Black" Muslims killed Malcolm X; Black Nationalists blame the "white man." A "white kid" wants to be an entertainer; conservatives blame N.W.A. Spanish fathers tell their daughters "Don't bring niggas in the house!" Black mothers tell their sons, "I betta not catch you with a white girl!" White fathers tell their daughters "You marry a spic and you're dead to me!" One thing these parents all seem to be is racist. One thing all these kids seem to be is niggers. Ask papi about his fascination with Beyonce, ask Ma about her love with Brad Pitt, and ask daddy dearest about his crush on Salma Hayek and then you'll hear, "Do as I say and not as I do!" Niggas are confusing.

This confusion led to the integration of "culture." Princes and princesses were forced to love their own, and because of this, they hated everyone that looked like them. "Like a thief in the night," sinners defied God. They broke the ultimate commandment, "Thou Shall Not Place Any Gods before Me!"

The "gods" were no more. There were only "mortals." This destroyed the "Gods" of the "holy trinity" Asia, Africa, and Europe. Eden was no more, ignorance was no longer bliss, and life was no longer beautiful. Eden became Sodom and Gomorrah, knowledge became power, and life became perfect.

(You ever wonder why "mixed babies" are more attractive than "pure bloods?" Because "half-breeds" are humans, "pure bloods" are gods. Think about it. In Olympia the gods promoted incest "to keep it all in the family" and scorned other gods who would have sex with mortals. Today, parents scorn their kids from dating outside their "race" and are encouraged to "keep it all in the family.")

Everyone hates to be perfect, no one wants to be imperfect but no one wants to admit their human.

"Jesus died to save men -- a small thing for an immortal to do, & didn't save many, anyway; but if he had been damned for the race that would have been act of a size proper to a god, & would have saved the whole race. However, why should anybody want to save the human race, or damn it either? Does God want its society? Does Satan?"

The same way "racist slave-owners" were forced to give up their mulattoes, is the same way "nigger slaves" were forced to give up theirs. The "mulattoes" were hated by the polarities of "race" because neither side wanted nothing to with them. The only thing respected by "whites" was the pure bloods "blonde hair blue eyes," the only thing respected by blacks were the Afro-centric "dark-skinned brother." The "blacks" like the "whites" both hated the "mulattoes," "mutts," and any other term used for "half-breeds." Like "Human Stains" the "half-breeds" had to constantly receive jealousy from both sides because of their omniscience in race. Some could pass for "white" and get good jobs; some passed for "blacks" and were allowed into Harlem club during the Renaissance, the "half-breed" was the distortion in illusion interruption, they were the "glitch in the matrix" they were the "non-existent" they were the niggers. The "half-breeds" were bred like ass backward mules that had no function but to serve the "gods." Black and White were the gods, grey was the mortal. So because these "Maureen Peals" were constantly judged by both sides, they hated both sides, they only held loyalty to themselves. Fuck black, fuck white, I'm ambiguous, I'm a nigger, I'm an enigma, I'm a sinner, and I'm human.

Black Panthers hated dope dealers and often fucked them up for selling junk to their people. Ku Klux Klan supported the Temperance movement and often fucked up bootleggers for selling junk to their people. However when "black dope dealers" sold in the white neighborhoods it was the "honkies' problem," it was the "guidos' problem" it was the "guineas' problem" it was the "kikes' problem" it was the "micks' problem" it was the "crackers' problem" it was no longer their problem. When "Italian, Irish, Jewish, and American bootleggers" were selling in the black neighborhoods it was the "eggplants problem" it was the "moolyans' problem" it was the "the niggers' problem" the "spades' problem" it was no longer their problem. Do you still wanna know history?

Once upon a time there was time there was a word named Black. Now no one liked Black because Black was the worst thing to be in the late 1800s and early to mid 1900s. Black symbolized depression, poverty, filth, and loneliness. Black killed millions in the 1800s with disease, Black destroyed the Stock Market, and Black holds things against you to get what it wants. It's easy to see that black had no friends. White however, was the shit! Whites' cake was heavenly, Whites' pasta was angelic, and White escorted women to weddings, because White was innocent. Everyone wanted to hang out with White because White had all the girls, all the criminals, all the athletes, all the entertainment, White had everyone and everything in check. Everyone would leave Black to go play with White. You weren't a good athlete unless you played sports with White, You weren't a good singer unless you sung with White, and you weren't a real criminal unless you were jailed with White. Anyone who is anyone wanted to be White. White was that nigga. The light-skin niggas were the closest friends to White that Black could hang with without getting beat up, so Black loved to be with light-skin niggas because White symbolized success. "I can't get Marylyn Monroe, fuck it, I'll settle for Etta James." So Grey began to be liked because they appealed to Black and resembled White.

But often Grey didn't want anything to do with Black because Black didn't want anything to do with Grey until they hung out with White. Before Grey met White they were ugly, before they met White they were lonely. But now that White knew Grey everyone wanted one. Being White became the fad for the times. Slicking hair, bleaching skin, wearing cardigan sweaters, listening to the Beach Boys, Elvis, Frank Sinatra, the Beatles, watching Marylyn Monroe, Shirley Temple, Rick Barry, Jerry West, Paul Arizin, Rocky Marciano, Al Capone and Bugsy Siegel, Rodney Dangerfield, John F. Kennedy, having a house with a white picket fence and a Golden Retriever in the lawn was all that came with hanging with White. But one day that would all change.

Niggas got tired of White. White became cliché, trite, White became whack. White was over-exposed and White's status hit the top, so the only thing left for White to do was to plummet. White was seen for what White was: just another nigga. White was caught on TV by the paparazzi sicking dogs on Black. Black was just the geek and White was the popular kid who gave Black wedgies with high-powered hoses and beating Black with batons. But that wouldn't destroy White's reputation just yet. People were shocked to see White do these things, so they asked White is it true? And at first White denied and said "You know that shit ain't true! Black is lying" But then White was caught slippin', White was caught tyrna kill Black. When niggas tried to stop White, White then attacked everyone that got in White's way. Grey left White because White turned on Grey before White died and told Grey "You're not me and you could never be me, go be Black!" So niggas fucked up White to save Black. In the 60s some nigga asked "Who gonna replace White? White was so cool, who's gonna fill that void?" Black answered "I will."

So, Black became that nigga. Stokely Carmichael screamed for "Black Power!" James Brown made niggas say "Black and I'm Proud" Syl Johnson asked Was it because he was Black Tommie Smith and John Carlos saluted Black at the Olympics in 1968 "Black is Beautiful" became the slogan around campus and everyone loved Black. Black now took out the perms and pompadours to put in Afros and Cornrows to distinguish themselves from White. Black hung out with Sidney Poitier, Jackie Robinson, Muhammad Ali, Bumpy Johnson, Nicky Barnes, Malcolm X, Martin Luther King Jr., Pam Grier, James Baldwin, Richard Pryor, Red Foxx, Wilt Chamberlain, Oscar Robinson, and Bill Russell. Black didn't wear cardigans, they wore black berets. Black wasn't listening to Beach Boys; Black listened to Marvin Gaye and Al Green. Black didn't live in suburbs they lived in the projects, they didn't have Golden Retrievers they had Rottweiler's. To be like Black, niggas stopped bleachin' their skin and started getting tans, they all grew their hair out and screamed "Fuck the man!" Grey was the closest thing White could get to Black without actually being Black. So White looked for Grey frequently. Grey remembered what White did and said "Remember when you said I wasn't White? Well I agree, fuck you White!"

When Grey came back around to like Black, Black told Grey "Oh now you like me? Fuck outta here; go be White!" Grey then said that White wanted nothing to do with them. Black told Grey "Well you ain't me either so be yourself." Light-skin was frowned upon and dark-skin became a signal for strength. Black had the game on lock but something happened.

White came back and starting spreading rumors about Black telling niggas that Black smoked crack and had AIDS. White then made niggas follow them with cameras to the projects and said "This just in" After Black was caught doing crack they became unpopular again. White, even though they used crack too, didn't show anyone and kept it a secret. White constantly pointed the finger of wrong doing by Black and said "Look at what Black does; I told you they were nothing." So again niggas left Black and went back to White.

Someone's probably asking "Where's Grey?" Grey did exactly what Black and White told Grey to do: be yourself. Grey became the President of the United States on January 20, 2009.

Don't you just love Happy Endings!

Black was a fad, just like White. The same way no one wants to be called "nigger" now is the same way no one wanted to be called "black" back then. But like all fads everyone is gonna want to be called "nigger" then after awhile that word is gonna get tired and then people are gonna start callin each other racist. And this will always happen because History always repeats itself. I know one thing, if people's great-great- great-great-grandparents were alive now and heard niggas accepting being called "black" they'd say "I don't understand your generation, something is wrong with the world today." Sounds familiar? Illusion Interruption. One thing I can say about Grey no matter how often they switch sides, they still manage to be accepted. I love niggas. Sometimes life isn't as black and white as people say it is, sometimes life is grey. (Damn I might've ruined an element to the book! Ahh well, niggas won't notice.)

Ooh! Ooh! History also has a slang meaning... Something that is no longer worth consideration. Think about that the next time you say, "Don't call me nigger, I'm black!"... **Nigga!!!**

If you wanna kill this word, kill yourself. That's bound to work.

Show
a

Is this a perfect world? Most of you will undoubtedly say no, but why? Most of you will then answer with your reasons, not realizing that they're *your* reasons. Although your opinions are highly welcomed and needed, I must ask another question; do you really know what the word perfect means? Not *your* concept or perception of perfect, but *the* meaning of perfect? Again, most of you will then say, "Well what's the difference?" There is a big difference between what *you* think is perfect and what perfect *actually* is. When looking at perfect we may say, "well, a perfect is world where no one is starving, everyone is rich and happy, and nothing bad happens to anyone." Now this may be *our* concept of perfect, but it is *really* what perfect means? Now I already know that most of you reading this will say "this is dumbest s#*'t I have ever read," but before you do, don't think, just read, because your initial response is usually the right one.

Perfect means to be entirely without fault or defect; it means to satisfy all requirements and is accurate in doing so. Perfect means faithfully reproducing the original perfection lacks no essential detail, making it complete, whole, impartial, unbiased, and unflawed. Imperfection however means defective: having one or the other, but never both; imperfection lacks sexual reproduction. Now, when you read this definition, reevaluate the question first stated. Were you thinking about *your* concept of perfect, or the actual meaning of *perfect*?

When answering this question earlier, you may have unconsciously answered with your opinion; that is expected, because that makes us human. When asked questions, we as a species don't think entirely about what's being expected of us as humans, we do what all humans do naturally: we give what we think of a situation, usually without asking and act accordingly. This is what the human race is based upon; we are a species whose innate ability is to survive by doing what *we* think. Rarely, do we ever think of the consequences that come with our actions, because it is our primal needs that incline us to do so, thus making us human. This is the reason why the human race is prone to mistakes scientifically, and is doomed to sin religiously. It is who *we* are.

No one is above this inclination, and no one is below this inclination, because it is already expected.

What most of you were thinking of when answering the question was a utopia. A utopia is an imaginary and indefinite remote place; it is a place of *ideal* perfection especially in laws, government and social conditions. Utopia is an impractical scheme for social improvement. That is the difference between *the* perfect world and *our* perfect world: the real world we actually live in is perfect, but the world in which *our* fantasies, indulgences, wants, desires, aspirations, ideas, and perceptions are our God is the utopia. The physical world is perfect; our mental world is imperfect. We should now understand that all of us are mentally living in a fantasy, but are physically acting out our mental fantasy in the real world; the human psyche is the ultimate psychopath. It is not our jobs to understand it; it is only our jobs to accept it.

From the moment we are born, we already have a complex mental process. However, no one can understand the mental process of another person, because we are our own entire person. There is only one law, which no one can refute, rebuke, deny, or discredit: human nature. No matter how strong, resilient, or evasive our minds are we are all inclined physically to do exactly what nature tells us to do; atheists, agnostic, Christian, Muslim, Catholic, heterosexual, homosexual, Jewish it doesn't matter, because we are all capable of doing the same things, because essentially, we are the same. If your stomach growls, you will eat if you have to use urinate, you will do so. There is nothing that the body tells you, which can be fought against. No matter how hard you try, you will always lose. Those who win, usually die. If your body is hungry and your mind is not, then you will try to fight the hunger, because your mind hasn't succumbed to the body, but eventually if you don't fulfill your body's purpose your body will fail you.

For example, supermodels are seen in society, as the most beautiful creatures mankind has to offer. They are usually the standard of what is beautiful and what is acceptable. Often because of this, most models are forced to uphold that standard by any means necessary. A strict diet is enforced for these models to uphold their image. Those who uphold this image may look beautiful to us, because it is a standard in which we aspire to become, but in reality, these models suffer intensive bodily and mental damage. In some cases models' diets are not correlated with what their body wants, but because they want to uphold this image they are willing to train their mind into believing that they don't need to eat like everybody else, because they are not everybody else. Models feel like they are better than everybody else, because they do not live like the majority. This is true in some cases, most models don't aspire to be normal people, but most normal people aspire to be models. When looking at a model we don't say they want to be like us, we say we want to be like them. This is why most celebrities are nasty to average people, because they feel that they are better, not because they are better, but primarily because we make them better. We place them above us and in doing this they have now supernatural powers. To us supermodels and celebrities are not regular they are super, not because they are super, but because we make them super. That is why it is such a shock to see so many supermodels suffer from bulimia, anorexia, depression, because to us they are not normal, they are super, but in reality they are just as likely to commit the same mistakes as us, because in reality they are normal.

"In equating physical beauty with virtue, she stripped her mind, bound it, and collected self-contempt by the heap."

This not only destroys the psyche of the models, but it destroys the psyche of humanity ten times more, because society has disobeyed the first commandment: "Do not have any other gods before me." This is the first offense toward God, because God made this world for us, but the sole purpose for our existence is not for *our* purpose but for Gods' purpose. God's greatest creation was the world and everything in it. When *we* look at the world on an individual basis, our vision is only *our* vision, and because of this *our* picture is always distorted. However, if you think outside the box and look at the world as whole entity, then you will see how perfect the world actually is, but most of humanity is unable to do so because humanity is based on individual thought, not collective thought. Although it is our individualism that makes us who we are, it is also *our* individualism that takes us away from reality.

Realistically, all of us at some point or another display psychopathic behavior we don't look at our behavior as psychopathic, but if you analyzed everything you've done, you will notice that it is. Most of our impulses come out of what we are compelled to do scientifically and religiously.

Religiously stating, all of mankind is compelled to sin. In the beginning of time, God made the world and everything in it in six days, on the seventh day he rested. This is the way that God has created the world; he worked six days and rested on the seventh. This is the suit that mankind was set to follow; live and learn for six days, but on the seventh day, reflect on all that you have learned and give praise to God, because God has placed the world here for us, but not for *our* purpose but for God's purpose. It is imperative that we understand that <u>*our only*</u> purpose is to serve God.

When God made man, God took the dust from the ground and molded him into his image. God then breathed air into his nostrils, giving man life, and this is when *our* history as a people begins. After_creating man, God placed man into the Garden of Eden; in this garden, God made two trees: the Tree of Everlasting Life, and the Tree of Knowledge of Good and Evil. The Tree of Everlasting Life is the tree which fruit bears everlasting life. The other tree, which is the Tree of Knowledge of Good and Evil, bears the fruit of conscious thought, eating from the Tree of Knowledge not only gives us consciousness, but also gives us a conscious knowledge that our actions are defined as either good or evil.

In the days following, God placed Adam into the Garden of Eden to work and keep it. While working, God told Adam that he is allowed to eat of all the fruit of the Garden except from_the Tree of Good and Evil, because God told Adam that "for in the day that you eat of it you shall surely die." God told Adam that if he can resist eating from the Tree of Good and Evil, then he may eat from the Tree of Everlasting Life and become one with God. God gave Adam the job to name all of the living creatures in the garden. It was at this time that God realized that Adam had no one to help him. In seeing this, God placed Adam into a deep sleep, and while Adam was asleep, God took one of his ribs and made woman. The man named woman "woman." because she came from the womb of a man. After woman was created God then told Adam that a "man shall leave his father and his mother and hold fast to his wife, and they shall become one flesh." This is the relationship of marriage, when we marry; we leave from our mother and father to become a part of another. When we are raised, are parents are perfect because whatever one parent lacks, the other compensates for. That's why it's normal to see that one parent is always more strict than the other, because they make the perfect balance; individually, a parent fails, but together they make the perfect equation, which is reproduction.

Now while there was complete happiness on the world, there was upheaval between God and Lucifer. God who was pleased with all of his work, rested, but Lucifer who hated man was displeased with all that has been done. Lucifer was God's favorite angel, because he was the most beautiful of all the angels in heaven. God's command was for Lucifer to serve Adam and Eve in the Garden of Eden, but because Lucifer was proud he declined, because he felt that he was better than God's creation. Lucifer, which means "bearer of light," represents our thoughts. Prior to Lucifer, Adam lived in complete happiness, because they live in ignorance. They knew nothing of the world, but what they were told, and that is why they were happy. Nothing ever went against Adam, because Adam and Eve didn't know the difference. The only thing that they knew is what God told them, and because they put complete faith in God, they reflected God's perfection. They never disobeyed God, because they never knew the difference. All that mankind could define them with, is their actions, but because these actions are what God dictated they followed him faithfully and never questioned God because they never thought, they only followed.

It should now be understood at this juncture, that Lucifer represents human cognition and individuality. When Lucifer rebelled against God, he divided himself from God and this is when the Fall of Man began. After, Lucifer was cast from God he then became Satan. From the son of light Lucifer transformed into the son of darkness. When Lucifer was with God, Lucifer was the angel who could think for him, but although he had the ultimate freedom, he did not allow that to divide him from God, because he loved God, because God loved him. Lucifer was the most beautiful angel of all because Lucifer was the only angel who could think for him, but he still followed God. This explanation shows the ultimate devotion, humility and faith between God and Lucifer. After God created mankind, Lucifer felt betrayed, because he felt that if anyone should be served it should surely be him. Lucifer in all his knowledge could not understand God's decision, and because Lucifer could not understand his decision he began to resent God, soon after hating God.

In Lucifer's pride he did not follow God's command he envied it. The reason Lucifer began hating God is because he *wanted* to be God. God already knew of this and cast Lucifer from heaven. Lucifer tried to overthrow God, but because God is all knowing, God destroyed Lucifer and his followers and they were sent to earth. Now I know that some of you reading this are saying, "Well why we are paying for something Lucifer did?" The reason is this is the ultimate test of love, devotion, faith, reverence, and humility towards God. Adam and Eve were created by God, but Adam and Eve never truly loved him, they only followed, God could never prove that we truly love him, so he decided to let us go; as stated earlier, it is not made to be understood, it is only made to be accepted.

There is a quote that states, "If you love somebody, let him or her go. If they return, they were always yours. If they don't, they never were." This is exactly what God has done; God loves all of us, and he loves us so much that he let us go, because God knows that those who love in return come back. Those who return are those who truly love him, and because they *truly* love him, they will reap the ultimate reward of everlasting life. Not everlasting life in *our* cognition of being physically 1,000 years old, but we will always be around even when no one can see us. And because God will always see us, the world will always see us, because the world will always see God. Those who don't see are those who don't believe, and those are the ones who don't love God. And because they don't love God, they don't love themselves, because they want to be God, and because they know that they can **never be God, it destroys all those who don't believe**.

Meanwhile in the Garden, after Lucifer was cast out of heaven, he was transformed into Satan. As Lucifer assumed his new identity through dissociative fugue as Satan, he no longer "bared light," he now bared darkness. Satan means "accuser," and when Satan whispered into Eve's ear, that is exactly what Satan did; he accused God of keeping man blind so that God could make the decisions for Adam and Eve. "The greatest trick the devil pulled on the world was making the world believe he didn't exist." Satan's strongest and most valued asset is his whisper, but he tricks us into believing that he doesn't exist, so that we could do what he wants. Satan wants mankind to divide from God; his whisper is so dangerous, because it makes us believe that it is we, but in reality it is Satan. However, that initial response in which all human nature is inclined to is God. Our "primal instinct" is God given, whereas our "humanity" is Satan.

Satan assumed the appearance of the serpent in most biblical stories for a reason, a serpent is a quiet creature capable of anything, and because a serpent is capable of anything, we undermine its ability to be dangerous. Unlike any other animal in the world, the snake has no limbs, but even in its harmless appearance it is still recognized as one of the most dangerous animals in the world. The serpent cannot grab you with arms, or pursue with legs, all a serpent can do is attract you with its harmless appearance. As you get closer, the serpent lulls us with their subtle hiss, which is like a siren to our demise. The temptation of the serpent is so intriguing because it *looks* harmless, but in reality it is not, a serpent should never be underestimated. When you've gotten within the grasp of a serpent, it no longer lulls you, the same harmless serpent attacks you, and if permitted, the serpent will kill you.

Satan killed all of us who live today; all of us who live today are dead to God. We don't live in God's world, which is reality; we live in Satan's world, which is fantasy. This fantasy is known as "individual perception:" this individual perception shows how we look at the world, and from then we start to compare ourselves to the rest of world making ourselves feel that we are better than what is already here. Now in *our* minds we feel nothing is wrong with this, but in reality God hates us for this. God made existence perfect holistically, not individually. But, because our "sanity" tells us that we are individuals, and not whole, we take away from what is already here: perfection.

Although woman was the first with thought, women are not the sole reason for sin being brought upon humanity. Sin as we all knew it, always existed but because Adam and Eve never knew the difference, there was only perfection. All that mankind ever knew before cognitive thought was what God taught. Before cognition there was no difference, there was only the same. Somehow, in God's graciousness mankind understood that even in similarity there is difference. This juxtaposition shows the complexity of God; humans have the intuitive ability to know without knowing, and those "gut feelings" is how God communicates with us. God knows that the mind will never accept him, because Satan holds our mind captive in fantasy, so God connects with us through our body. This is what makes us all God's creatures because no matter how much we try to dissent from each other. God will always connect us, because essentially we are all connected.

Before Eve ate from the tree, she then convinced Adam to think the same way in which she thought; she told Adam what she was told by the serpent and then they carried out the ultimate sin. Now, even at this point is Adam nor Eve fully aware of their actions, because at this point they don't know the difference between God and Satan. They are still following what they are being told, because Adam and Eve are still ignorant. Before I continue any further, it is important that you understand that even though Satan split from God, Satan and God are undoubtedly the same entity. For God to divide humanity from the world, God had to first divide himself, because God reflects the world and the world reflects God, so when God casted Lucifer from Heaven, he casted mankind from paradise. In the realist form of reality God took away to give to us, but because we were cast from God, we subconsciously resent him, and because we are not consciously aware of this, we openly disrespect God. For God to make the perfect test God had to make the perfect sacrifice, perfection; God had to take away from perfection to contribute to ours. And ever since then, we have been trying to create *our* own perfection, by taking away from God's perfection. In reality, we are trying to play God, and that's the purpose of individualism; to make *you* feel like you have control, but this is only what *you* feel, because in reality you have *no control*, and because no one has control, everyone has control, and that is perfect, because everyone is God and God is everyone; not individually but holistically.

As for Adam and Eve, they were not deceived or mislead, they did exactly what they were told to do: disobey. God was the serpent in the Garden, and because of this he awoke man from their ignorance, and freed their mind from happiness. Now when reading the bible or hearing of biblical stories, it is implied that we were deceived somehow, but in the realist form of reality we obeyed his command. To understand that, you must understand that there is no difference between Satan and God, because they are one. There was never any difference because there was never any similarity, and because there was never any similarity, there was only perfection; perfection lacks nothing, because it has everything. Adam and Eve were told by God to not eat from the Tree of Knowledge of Good and Evil, but God knew that as soon as that command was given it was Adam and Eves' naturally inclination to go against authority. In the realist form of reality, Adam and Eve always had free thought and free choice, but they confided it in God. God was pleased with their loyalty so he decided to give humanity the ultimate freedom: to divide themselves from God. In God doing this, he allowed man to become God.

When God made the Garden he instructed Adam to do things, and because Adam and God were one, he never disobeyed. But when God warned Adam about the Tree of Knowledge, God already knew that because it was not instructed and warned of Adam to not eat from the Tree, it was the first time in which man would have to decide from himself what was right and wrong. There is a difference between instruction and warning; instruction means to teach, to give knowledge to, and to make a demand of directly. However, a warning is to call to ones attention, it is to counsel; a warning is to inform someone, not teach someone. That was the difference, people rarely go against teachings, but we often go against warnings.

Every time we are taught something, we humble ourselves to the teachings. In actuality, we begin to resent the teacher because we feel the teacher has undermined us, and we start to think that the teacher believes that we are incapable of making our own decisions. When this happens, our humility feels betrayed and then we learn to watch the mistakes of the teacher; if we see one fault in the teachers' instruction, we then begin to separate ourselves from the teacher's teachings making us our own person. When we divide ourselves, we then become proud because we have made a promise to never follow the steps of the teacher, and only follow what we believe. This is when individualism begins.

On the other hand, if the teacher warns us instead of teaching us we often disregard the teacher initially, and feel that the teacher is stupid, because in our minds they don't know what they're talking about. We divide ourselves from the beginning, and decide that we are our own person; when this starts, our pride begins to engulf our sanity now believing that we are the only one capable of "logical" choices. Our pride blinds us, and we tend to drift further and further and further away from the teacher. In actuality, we are only doing what the teacher wanted us to do, which is give us a head start, and counsel. This teacher has not instructed, this teacher has warned, and this is why we deviate, because we undermine the knowledge of foreshadow the teacher has. When we come back in terms with realist of reality, we realize that our teacher was correct. This realization destroys *our* sanity, which is known as our pride and makes us twice as humble as we were before. In our humility, we run right back to where we came: the teacher. "If you love somebody, let them go. If they return, they were always yours. If they don't, they never were." God loved Adam, because Adam loved God; Adam and God are one, just as Eve and Satan are one, but holistically they are perfect. I cannot *instruct* you to think, I can only *warn* you. It's not for to understand, it's for you to accept.

When God put Adam asleep, God fell asleep also. When he awoke, Satan was made and so was Eve. God is the ruler, Satan is the follower;

Adam is the ruler, Eve is the follower. Man represents God's ability to do; Woman represents Satan's ability to think. What I must emphasize is that there is no difference between the two, because they are one. I know there will be misogynists who will read this and feel superior, and I know there will be feminists who read this same paper and feel inferior and disrespected. The purpose is not praise one or the other the purpose is to praise both; this world needs the pride of man to compensate for the pride of woman, and this world needs the compassion of woman to compensate for the aggression of man. It is sad to see that this is undoubtedly a world organized by the patriarch, but even the kings of the wealthiest nations knows they need a woman to keep that kingdom. The matriarch is the warning and the patriarch is the teaching. The mother warns, the father teaches; the father chastises and the mother soothes. From one you will run to another, and from the other you will run back; that is perfection. It's not for you to understand; it's for you to understand, through this understanding it is now for you to accept.

When Adam was instructed to not eat from the Tree of Knowledge of Good and Evil, he then resented his own instruction. In his resentment, he rested on the seventh day, which was the day he slept. During his sleep he fought with Lucifer, which was cognitive thought and that's when the division of perfection began. When God and Lucifer split, man and woman did, because our mental split in the realist of all realities, and because our bodies split in the fantasy of all fantasies, man and woman were no longer one. The perfect test requires the perfect division, and the perfect division illustrates the perfect imperfection. This perfect imperfection is excellence not individually, holistically. Now when Adam and Eve ate from the Tree of Knowledge of Good and evil, they began not only to think, but they also became able to define which thoughts were "good" and which ones were "bad."

Their initial thought was to look at each other's body. When looking at each other, Adam and realized that they were different; and because they **knew** the difference, they resented their difference and began to hate each other. When God saw this and told Satan "Because you have done this, cursed are you among all animals and among all wild creatures; upon your belly you shall go, and dust you shall eat all the days of your life. I will put enmity between you and the woman and between your offspring and hers; he will strike your head, and you will strike his heel." **Then God told Eve** "I will greatly increase your pangs in childbearing; in pain you shall bring forth children, yet your desire shall be for your husband, and he shall rule over you." **Finally he told Adam** "Because you have listened to the voice of your wife, and have eaten of the tree about which I commanded you, You shall not eat of it", cursed is the ground because of you; in toil you shall eat of it all the days of your life; thorns and thistles it shall bring forth for you; and you shall eat the plants of the field. By the sweat of your face you shall eat bread until you return to the ground, for out of it you were taken; you are dust, and to dust you shall return." **This is when man's** conscious knowledge of failure begins: the original sin.

To understand what happened in the most general sense, you must be human. Knowing, that everyone reading this paper is human, it is only fair that I continue. The original sin in which all mankind is inclined to is sexual intercourse; no man or woman can refute sexual desire for it is the ultimate desire in which all mankind wants. The only thing that separates us is the way we perceive it, but in reality, sexual intercourse is necessary for mankind to continue. And because man has pride, he will not allow himself to be defeated, so in his proud actions, he has sex to preserve his perfection, but because he was already perfect, he has just created something imperfect. That is why marriage is so important in every culture, because the intrinsic value of marriage is perfection. When you "marry" you have decided that you as a couple are perfect, and because you are perfect, you now realize that you must pass on your perfection. This passing on refers to reproduction; the only way to reproduce is to have sex. And that is the sin in which no one can rebuke, because it rebukes itself. Marrying the way we understand it is going to the church to blessed and having brides and grooms, eating cake and dancing. In the realist of all realities, that is only the "courting" period in which you have decided you want to defy God. The whole time we are looking for our soul mate, we are subconsciously, looking for someone who if we died tomorrow, there is something of your perfection that can be passed on, something that can be preserved.

Religiously, we're saying that if I'm going to defy God, I want to do it with someone I hate, because I already love myself.

That's why those who hate themselves can never love another person because they don't love God. And because they don't love God, God doesn't love them. God is the tests of all tests; no one can look at their complete opposite, their mortal enemy and not say they love them. The reason they can say they love the other is because they subconsciously hate themselves. And because they subconsciously hate themselves they openly project hate onto the other person, but when they awake from their fantasy, they realize that they love the person more than they actually love themselves. When this happens, they successfully "sin" and that's how perfection continues. It is a part of who we are. It is for you to understand, not to accept.

In Eden, when God told Adam to not eat of the Tree of Knowledge, Adam was telling himself to not have sex with Eve. So for six days he works to avoid the temptation of Eve, because he hates Eve but subconsciously but doesn't know it. He hates Eve because he thinks Eve is he, and because Adam secretly hates himself, he hates Eve. On the seventh day, he realizes that Eve is not he she is separate from him. He realizes this, because on the seventh day he decided to have sex with her. When he fell asleep after having sex, he realized that Eve was so different that she was the same. As he awoke he rebuked himself, his thoughts, and his wife, because he realized that trying to multiply perfection only made him human.

As for Eve, she was always there, but Adam always overlooked her because he was too proud to ever admit she was there. Because he was too proud to admit this, he defeated himself quicker, because he instructed and didn't warn himself; ultimately he fought against himself and lost. Adam commanded himself to not eat of the "forbidden fruit." which was Eve and Adam felt that if he could successfully do so, that would make him God. In reality, no one is God, so all Adam was committing was the sins of all sins; Adam did not want to accept the fact that he was human. And because he could not be God, hates himself, he hates woman, and he hates his nature. The original sin is sex, because it humbles mankind's pride and makes them realize that they need something that they lack to produce something better, and that destroys the way we think of ourselves, because we realize that we're not God we are only human. At this point I would expect two reactions: either the paper is the floor, or you're looking to read on. Most of you will read on because it was said as counsel and not instruction. Pride doesn't respond well to instruction, it responds well to counsel. Even if you have thrown this paper into the garbage, something in you wants to know where this is going, because you want to prove I'm wrong. So what you will do is read to say that I'm stupid, but all you will be doing is rebuking yourself. Because I love you, I'll let you go because I know those who love me back will return and keep reading.... "God's will, shall be done"

For those of you who have continued to read I love you just as much as you're reading this paper. Back to Eve, she was never noticed because Adam denied her existence, so she resented Adam. In her resentment, she began to study Adam; she learned his likes and dislikes, but never allowed Adam to know this, because he was too proud. Eve was humble, she admitted that she loved Adam, but she could never get Adam to admit it because he felt he was better than her. This eventually made her hate him, but the only reason she hated him is because she loved him and he didn't love her. So through humility, Eve became the serpent of the "Garden." She is serpent, who has the power to seduce, and look harmless, but with malicious intent she knew she would destroy Adam's paradise of innocence, with reality. Eve knows that no matter how much Adam thinks he doesn't need her, she will *make* him need her.

On the six days in which man created the world and everything in it, Eve watched. She watched how Adam took pride in his work, and how he took credit for all of it, discounting her efforts because he was too proud to admit that he needed help. During the week when Adam was with all that made him proud Eve seduced him, not with pride, but with humility. She became the ultimate demise of man's godliness. Eve knew that Adam hated anything different, because he loved himself proudly. Even though Eve could not fully understand it she accepted it. She was not separate from Adam, she became Adam, and because she became Adam, Adam loved her. She didn't have her own voice, she had *his* voice, she sounded like him, moved like him, after a while she became him, but in reality she knew she could never be him, because they are whole. She could never pull Adam away from his work, because Adam's work reflected him, and because Adam believed he was perfect, he thought everything he produced was perfect, and because Eve never defied him, he was left ignorant, and because he was left ignorant, he was happy. Eve decided that this could not go on a second longer.

On the seventh day, Adam and Eve were talking, and Adam asked Eve if the world was perfect. She knew that the world was not perfect, because he did not produce this world by himself. She knew that if she lied to him, it would only destroy him further making him believe he was God. At first she didn't answer, Adam asked again "Tell me the truth Eve, isn't the world perfect?" Eve asked gently "you want the truth?" He replied sternly "Yes." Being offended she replies "the truth, you couldn't handle the truth." In his defense he begins to attack Eve, because he feels insulted. He asks her one more time "Is the world perfect?" She looks at him harmlessly at first, then her facial features sharply transformed into the man's worst nightmare; Eve told man the truth, "No!" That destroys Adam and makes him hate her forever. She has done one thing that is the forbidden rule of all men, make them gods with lies, and make the human with truth. That is man's first commandment to woman; don't put anybody else before me. In reality, man lacks the reciprocity, which makes it whole; and this is how imperfection came to be.

When Adam awoke from what he thought was a nightmare, he realized the truth. He needed a woman to preserve his "perfection," and because of this he hated himself. He did not want to take away from his "perfect" world because he knew he would have to give his "perfection" to his "imperfect" seed, and that killed him, not holistically but individually. Man's concept of sin is humility. Man finds it hard to place himself below who he thinks he's better than, and because of this God destroyed

Adam with the truth. The reason why, is because man started to believe that he was better than what he really was, and because it was God who allowed man to believe that it is only right that God tells the truth. The truth we all hate to hear is "WE ARE NOT GOD, WE WILL NEVER BE GOD, AND THE MORE WE TRY TO BECOME GOD, THE MORE WE SHOW OUR DISDAIN FOR GOD, AND BECAUSE WE SHOW WE HATE GOD, GOD WILL SHOW US HE HATES US, BY TELLING US THE TRUTH" and the truth is we are not God; we are human. Enjoy it, and for those who enjoy it God bless you, but for those who fight it, your world will be destroyed in this life or the next. I don't care if you understand, I don't care if you accept, but you will testify.

Adam, disgusted with what he has done destroyed Eve. He blamed her for his imperfection, but in the realist of realities she woke him up from his fantasy. Now we are all aware that Adam and Eve are from the same flesh, so to us it is disgusting for us to think that Eve had sex with Adam. Sorry to disappoint all of you who are "innocent" but Adam had sex with his sister. If you're not willing to accept that Adam had sex with his biological sister, then accept that in the eyes of God we are all brothers and sisters. Most people who study the bible know this, and that's why parents try to separate the sons from the daughters; parents know that kids are innocent, and because they're innocent they feel they must they "protect" them. By protection I mean not allowing boys to see girls naked and vice versa. The only reason why most parents won't allow their children to wash up together is because they know that kids will try to have sex. Most parents will never admit this to children because they feel they are protecting them.

In reality, God shows parents that no matter how hard you try to control your children they will leave you. If it will happen then it will undoubtedly happen. That is God's will, "no matter what you do, I will always get my way, because my way is everyone else's way, and because my way is everyone else's way, everyone else's way is my way, and my way is my will, and my will, shall be done." That is the pain of parenting, knowing no matter how hard you try you cannot control what you've made. Parents always try to play God, because when you encounter complete innocence for the first time it is beautiful that you feel you must do "anything" to protect this innocence. This anything means you will attempt everything, because your limits are endless in protecting what is yours. In reality, everything really means nothing because no matter what you do you cannot control your child. That's why parents end up depressed, because when they realize that they cannot control children they begin to live, not individually but holistically.

That is the mortal fight for mankind, to be like God. We are all fighting this battle of trying to be like God, but we will never be God and that kills us, not holistically but individually. The bible is not supposed to be read literally, it's suppose be read figuratively. The Holy Bible is not a book of instructions; it is a book of warnings. The bible makes people become more human, by making people believe they're godlier. People take a book of poetry and try to live out poetry in reality. A lot of people who read the book of Genesis are actually looking for a Tree of Everlasting Life. There is no real Tree of Everlasting Life, that's why it has yet to be discovered because that tree doesn't exist. None of those stories in the bible are literally true. These are personal accounts of life where everyone searches for a meaning and finds out that life is no different from anyone else's because life is to be lived holistically not individually.

For those who really read the bible you know that none of the stories in there are any different from anything else you encounter in life. That's why priests, rabbis, pastors, and reverends can control people with the bible, because they know just as much as the people being controlled that there is no difference between someone who controls and someone being controlled, there is no difference. Control is an illusion of perspective; control depends upon the person, they use their perspective to decide whether they're controlling or being controlled, essentially there is no difference. If you miss a shot in a basketball game, you may make every possible analysis to understand why you missed but it doesn't change the fact that you missed. You trying to "control" past actions cripples your success in the future. If you are trying to control something that has already happened in the past then you have learned nothing. You cannot change anything that has already happened.

God is not a name, it's a title. God is the highest Supreme Being that controls everything around us. No one is above God; no one goes against God, because God smites all that smites God. Now reading the bible gives you a spectacular perspective of how life on this world came to be, it also gives you a well detailed explanation of why we are to follow the rules of God, and what happens when we don't follow these rules. Now when you read these stories of the bible it is imperative that you don't read with critique because the bible is undoubtedly the truth, all of these stories have significant meaning to the reader; whatever the reader decides to take out reflects the readers' understanding of life.

It becomes a problem when someone teaches the bible because it breeds antagonism in the student. When the bible is read individually, the understanding depends solely on the reader. There is no pressure on the reader, because the reader is not "controlled" by the bible, the reader controls the bible. It's a different thing when you are taught the bible. When you are taught the bible it is imperative that you understand the bible the way it is taught and nothing else. When you are taught the bible, you're forced to see things that are not there. Because the bible is poetry in its highest form, it is the most dangerous book in the entire world. No one can actually prove that these stories are real so these stories can be manipulated for something that they are not. If someone is uncertain in their interpretations of the bible then they may keep their perspective of the bible to themselves, but if someone who reads the bible becomes dogmatic in teaching then they can control anyone they want to. The Holy Bible is no joke, atheists laugh at reasoning of God worshippers but it is important to realize that you will die if you're uncertain of the bible. Countries, empires, nations, and societies have been destroyed by this book. What's even more interesting, the same Holy Bible that caused Constantine to kill Jews during his campaign is the same book that freed the people of Israel from Egypt. This book frees and enslaves at the same time, this is the book of Everlasting Life.

Reciprocity, manners, rules and guidelines are illusions set to make you feel like you have control. When you walk on a train platform and someone bumps into you may immediately feel "violated" or "abused."

Now if the person who has just bumped you says nothing of the past event then you feel offended, but if that person says "sorry" then you feel better. Why? That person still bumped you but because you heard a verbal affirmation you feel better? Is that really what you feel or is that what you have been programmed to feel. Even now you feel offended reading this, but why? If you were never raised with "manners" then you would have never cared if someone bumped you because you know that saying sorry doesn't change anything.

What do they tell a man that has just served 7 years for a crime he didn't commit?

"Sorry"

Truth is we are all computer programs built for the "bigger purpose." All of us are software made for a specific purpose, we decide the purpose but it is society which defines the purpose. Think about everything you have ever done in life, were you doing what you wanted or you told to do what you wanted? What's the difference? Exactly, there is none. There is no difference between doing what you want and being told to do what you want, it's all an illusion built to make you feel like you can control your actions. In the realist of realities you cannot control action, action controls you.

"What the fuck am I talking about?" You know exactly what I'm talking about, and that's what scares you. Reality is a labyrinth of fantasy, and fantasy is a labyrinth of reality. "This writer isn't talking about shit." If that's the truth then why have you read this much? Don't even try to answer because there is none? Nigger defines ignorant "black" people, and nigga defines ignorant people. There is no difference between a black person and a white person, no matter how hard you try to see a difference you will never see any, because essentially there is none. That's why the word will never die, because that word never lived. Niggers don't die, and niggas don't either.

Nigger is not a person it's a word, just a word. Niggers aren't born, they're bred. You really believe niggers exist? Well if you believe that then you must believe that X-Men have an academy where a man in a wheelchair can tell you what you're thinking. Nigger is a self-fulfilling prophecy, psychologically stating. You're not born a nigger; you're told you are a nigger. Niggers are incapable of societal happiness; niggers can't understand society because society is told not to understand niggers. Think about it, really think, do you honestly believe niggers were just "born?" If you do then you must be a nigger as well.

You're going to tell me that you were born a slave who does not have control over there own body? Bullshit! That's what they were you told, that's what all "niggers" were told. All "niggers" are told that they will *never* become anything; *they* are all ugly, stupid, and incapable of reasoning. If you believe this then I'm sure you can explain the success of every person who has contributed to the prosperity of the world. America, Antarctica, Mexico, Italy, Africa and all across the seven seas there is no such thing as failure; there is no such thing as failure because there is no such thing as success, these concepts are defined by perspective not by action. You think that a slave knows that he is a slave; do you think Michael Jordan believes he's one of the greatest basketball players in the world? If you said yes, then you're thinking too much. A slave does not believe they're a slave, they think they are what they are: everybody else. It's not until someone else tells a slave that he's a slave, shows the slave the difference between being a slave and not being a slave does the slave actually realize what they really are. Michael Jordan didn't consider himself one of the greatest men that ever played the game, all he knew is he played basketball. Everyone else called him "greatness" he called himself exactly what he was: a man who played basketball.

Why do you think you never remember in detail yourself as a baby? It's because you never understood what you did, you just did it. Life was never defined for you, you defined life. You never did what you were told; you were told what you did. That's why we love to see pictures of ourselves as babies because otherwise we feel inadequate about our existence. We love to hear stories of our childhood because we are defined by society. We understand that from the day we are born, we are seen by the world as special, gifted, talented, and extraordinary. That doesn't exist to us when we are a baby, that is why none of us remember it. Being a baby is just like being in the Garden of Eden because the Garden of Eden doesn't exist just like our early childhood doesn't exist. It doesn't become a reality until we are told that it was a reality, because there is no such thing as reality.

No one can prove their own existence. If I'm lying then feel free to throw this paper to the ground. You know like I know that nothing in this world can be proved. That's why there will never be anything that no one can agree upon, because nothing actually exists. You think I'm crazy, I know you do because that's what you felt when you first starting reading. The whole time you're reading you're saying to yourself "where the fuck is he getting this shit from?" If you're feeling that way, you're now going to prove to me that you weren't feeling that way all along. The reason you don't feel that way is only because I said it first. Now what you're trying to do is prove everything I'm saying is wrong by proving that everything you're saying is right. What I will now ask you, what is right and what is wrong?

Right is defined by being in accordance with what is good, just and proper; right constitutes qualities of ideal morality and merit of social approval. Wrong however is defined as injurious, unfair, or unjust; wrong is an act inflicting harm to someone else without due provocation or just cause. The reason why I defined both is because we all use words that we never truly understand. We are always told what things mean without ever finding out for ourselves and because of this we never understand life. Be honestly honest, do you have a good explanation for everything you do. When asked why you did something, you answer with "Because I felt like it." but when you are asked "Why?" a second time you then begin to think about the action. That's when we all hear "I don't know."

"What's the use you learning to do right, when it's troublesome to do right and ain't no trouble to do wrong, and the wages is just the same?"

It is alright to admit that because that's what makes us all human, we all know that we don't *really* know anything. From the moment our parents recognize us as theirs, our world starts to be defined by them. We are told what is right and wrong, we told what is different and what is similar, we become our parents for the first four years of our life; it is not until we start school for the first time that our world becomes conflicted. We are no longer surrounded by familiarity, we are now lost in existence, because in our minds we don't know the difference. That's why kids cry the very first day of school. They are raised with specific rules that correlate with what their parents want. They know nothing beside what their parents tell them, so it is the parents' job to define how a child should act in society, because it is society that defines how the parent behaves with their children.

"Your father does not know how to teach. You can have a seat now.' I mumbled that I was sorry and retired meditating upon my crime."

There is no such thing as individuality because there is no such thing as society, because you can't have one without the other that means that both don't exist. Nothing can stand by itself, you can't have a winner without a loser and because of this you will never know the difference. If you were never told of the concepts of winning then you would never understand the losing, all you would see is action. Actions equate everyone, because everyone equates action. Everyone in the world is connected at the same time in the same way; we are all human, and because of our humanity we all produce the same things. However, it is only *our* perspectives that change these actions.

"Better to reign in hell, than serve in heav'n"

Nothing stated here is new or original. "That's the nice thing about carrousels, they always play the same songs." We all know this, but if we all know this then why is there so much division in the world? Perspective, it is our lifeblood, our medulla oblongata, our heart, our soul, our daily bread, perspective is our livelihood. Our perspective dictates the way we see the world. Even though we all know that the world stops for no one, we still need our perspective to produce to the continuity of the world. Without perspective you have to realize that there is no action. If we didn't think about actions there would never be actions, there would be nothing. That emptiness, that uncertainty, that insecurity, that realization that nothing is there forces you to adapt perspective. This perspective makes you see the world differently, not as a reality but as a fantasy. Whatever an action doesn't explain, your perspective can, that's why you love your perspective, and it's your perspective which makes you *feel* like you're in control. Your perspective makes you feel like God, not holistically but individually. Be Aware! Just know that your perspective is only your perspective and because it is only *your* perspective, your perspective only changes your world, no one else's.

"The mind is its own place, and in itself, can make a Heaven of Hell, a Hell of Heaven."

When we begin to experience the world though our perspective, it is no longer the same world, it now becomes *our* world. In our world we define what we want. This is the reality that all children live in; children believe that they can fly, be multi-billionaires, Power-Rangers, whatever children believe they want to do, they can do it. It's not until parents destroy *our* reality with *their* reality that we no longer believe in ourselves. People who limit others only limit themselves. When you tell anyone they can't do something, you're only projecting your abilities onto them. You're not crippling their capabilities; you're only crippling your own. For those who believe other people, you have not been crippled by society; you have allowed yourself to be crippled by society. No one can ever tell you anything that you don't know; when you realize this, there's nothing that you won't be able to do.

You think a blind person knows that they're blind? No, they're told repeatedly that they're blind, and because of this constant reality they become blind. We are always told what we are incapable of from the time we are born. "You can't do this, you can't do that." We are no different because we grow up believing it. Most children sole purpose is to fulfill the fate of the parent. Children are made to make up for the mistakes of the parent; if we're not here to compensate for past mistakes then we're here to ensure future success, either way, children are not their own person, they're their parents. We are molded, programmed, sculpted and designed by our parents to produce the functions that they want us to produce. Children are here for the parent's discretion, not for themselves; children are property, slaves, commodities and livestock bred for the prosperity of the parent.

All parents know this and this is why the children of the future always rebuke the past. Advancement in technology, nature, science, knowledge only exists because we are already programmed to do so. Whatever our parents didn't achieve in their life, they want us to fulfill. The reason for this, because they have "died" and can no longer do what they want, we have the "obligation" to give them what they missed out on. We have already been programmed with guilt. Since having guilt uploaded into our hard drives, our function is to now do whatever our parents say. Anyone familiar with history knows exactly what's coming next. "This sounds exactly like slavery." You said it, not me.

Slavery is a physical ailment as well as a mind state. No one and I will repeat in bold italics ***No one can make you do what you don't want to.*** If you did something then you did it, there is no such thing as you were made to do it. If you really didn't want to do something then you would take any consequence that would come with it, because you don't care. Slavery is mind state where you think like another person, you do whatever the person tells you because to you they make you do what you do. They oversee all your actions; they know what you're thinking before you're even capable of producing the exact same thought. As kids, we are frightened of our parents for this reason. We don't understand why we fear our parents, we just do. Parents know this because being a kid in 400 B.C. is no different as being a kid in 2008.

Parents that cripple their children only cripple themselves. If you see a "dumb" child, then you automatically know they have "dumb" parents. Intelligence doesn't reflect a person's capabilities, it reflects their limitations. If you see a "dumb" child then that means that their parents have limited them to a point which doesn't allow them to think beyond the boundaries that they are given. When you see a "smart" child, it means that the parents have not given them explicit boundaries. When children have no boundaries, then the child has no limitations on the things they can learn. "Dumb" children are given so many boundaries, that when they finally get freedom everything they do have to be extreme. They're not satisfied with small success; they are only pleased with the extremes, because they have been deprived for so long. "Smart" kids are given so little instruction, that they are forced to learn for themselves, this develops their brains ten times more than the average child. Although every culture and sub-culture have specific definitions on what makes a child "smart" or "dumb" these two types of children are raised the same way.

The "smart" kid is the kid who has little parenting. They never had much instruction, they compensate for their lack of traditional instruction with experience. Children that lack parenting tend to do what they want. "Smart" children are always into something, they don't have the stories of their parents past endeavors so they rely solely on their own experience. They may be wrong in some of their assertions, but their curiosity for finding the truth is what shows them different perspectives for one action. They don't settle for their perspective only, they want everyone's and anyone's perspective. The inquisitive mind of the "smart" kid is quarrelsome to adults. But at the same time its "smart" children that admit they are not know-it-alls. So often they hold their "humble" attitude. They take nothing personal when it comes to right or wrong, because all they want is the experience itself, they just want other perspectives as a means of comparison.

A "smart" kid becomes stoic for others' opinions because it doesn't change the experience; they just want the different viewpoints for whenever they feel like using it against people. The "smart" kid knows without knowing, they rely on human inclination. They follow what they're bodies tell them and nothing else. This may seem troublesome to society, but society secretly envies the "smart" kid because the "smart" represents everything that society isn't: free. "Smart" kids come and go as they please, they don't know different or debt, they only know what they see, nothing. "Smart" kids don't care what the world sees, because "smart" kids don't live in a world with rules, they live in a world where everything happens for a reason, whether they understand it or not, they know that their understanding has nothing to do with events and they accept it.

"Smart" kids become outsiders in "acceptable" society. They tend to not care about the opinions of others because they know that the majority is only following instructions. They dictate what makes them happy. No matter what society defines as success or failure, it will always be the "smart" kids that determine their own success.

However, the "dumb" child is the star in society. They are the child who receives praise. The "dumb" child receives credit, because society loves the "dumb" child. The dumb child is decorated with awards, medals, badges, and degrees because otherwise they feel inadequate. The "dumb" child is obsequious to the wants of society. Because of this they are openly rewarded.

They listen to whatever they are told. They're told to jump, they jump; they're told to read, they read. These kids won't go beyond what they are told, because all they know is what they are told. These are the kids if you told them nothing, they will do nothing. Their function lies totally within society. If a social norm requires drowning females that can read, they'll do it. If a social norm requires killing serfs, they'll do it. If a social norm requires pouring milkshakes on protesters, they'll do it. These "dumb" kids are the "smart" ones in the eyes of society.

"Obedience is better than sacrifice."

When "dumb" kids are following, "smart" kids are leading. When "smart" kids are revolutionizing, "dumb" kids are rebelling. "Dumb" kids bring facts; "Smart" kids bring experience. But one thing about kids, when it's time to play, they'll undoubtedly play. No matter how "dumb" or "smart," "black" or "white," "nigger" or "racist" these kids may seem to be, leave them alone and you'll see how kids really are. Just alike in every way. But you know who always changes this? The parents, kids see unity, parents see division. Divide and Conquer is the name of the game folks.

Psychologists will call me a psychopath; Religion will say I'm an
Anti-Christ; Philosophers will call me Skeptic, the government
will call me terrorist, Niggas will call me racist, Racists will call me
nigger, Homophobes will say I'm gay, Gays will call me androgynous,
Humanity will call me crazy, Adults will call me immature.

What's the difference? The niggas who believe them.

Call me whatever you want, I call myself "Misunderstood."

"It's funny. All you have to do is say something nobody understands
and they'll do practically anything you want them to."

"After all the highways, and the trains, and the appointments, and the
years, you end up worth more dead than alive."

Praying to God is expected, but is it expected for God to answer?

You

e

When "American Slavery" began, it was a "white's man nightmare." Africans, who were brought over for economic purposes, did not want to be slaves. Initially, "Africans" were not the best slaves. They grew up in Africa. There wasn't any tobacco and cotton picking in Africa, but there was a whole lot in America. A 21-year-old African that was raised to hunt would not take kindly to picking cotton. In reality, these Africans were destroying the "white mans" economic long-term goals. You had Africans rebelling: they were jumping off the boats, running away from the plantations and fighting back. You cannot make someone who was raised 31 years with the name Ahmed and in 2 days change his name to Walter; only a nigger would try that. Imagine if someone came in your house right now and said, "Your name is no longer Cheryl, it's now Diane." You would flip the fuck out! (Well you'll probably laugh first)

If you grew up thinking 2+2=4, and I took you to a country that said something else, how would you react? When an illusion interruption is shifted off its axis, "it could destroy the consciousness of a person leading them to confusion, displacement and insanity."

So you can probably piece together that the first generation of slaves was not with the picking cotton thing. Africans would rather die than be called English names, wear clothes and pick cotton. The word "nigger" was the last thing on their minds because I gotta say something: Africans couldn't speak English, so they didn't care about being called "niggers." They were more focused on getting the hell out of America and back to Africa. Now of course the "white man" would call the African a barbarian because Africans didn't wanna do something they've never been exposed to before. Ironically, the reason why "Africans" were brought over is because "Europeans" didn't know what the fuck they were doing either. Africans were "barbaric" because they didn't wanna wear clothes. Last time I checked it's hot as hell in Africa. The second reason for the "African" being "barbaric" was because they couldn't understand English. Mind you these are the same "civilized" people who refuse to allow "Africans" to read and write. I think the barbarian

119

is vivid in this description. Those who follow reflect those who lead. Illusion interruption.

The "white man" now had to find a substitute. There were white slaves, but the "proud black man" won't admit that, he'll say they were called "indentured servants" so there's a difference. Whatever floats your boat black man! Wait! "Blacks" hate boats.

Because "Africans" were already used to the contact of "Europeans," they were perfect. Originally, Africans came over in boats and had "freedom." The "Europeans" had it in their mind that "Africans" would help them build a country so they brought Africans over. But the first Africans didn't like to work because they were used to Africa. So slave-owners no longer paid attention to the illusion interruption of the past, they focused on the reality intervention of the present, the kids. Slave-owners realized that they couldn't make a grown ass man do whatever so they shunned the parents and focused on the children. That's what the auctions were for.

The auctions basically separated reality intervention from illusion interruption. This displaced the children from the parents. So the next generations of Africans were raised to pick cotton, wear clothes and not read and write. And because these children were **raised** to do this, they had no problem. They didn't believe they were slaves, they just believed they were **niggaz.** They never been in Africa, all they knew was the antebellum south, so basically history defaulted itself. I was exposed to hearing, "no homo" and now I say it all the time, does that make me a homophobe?

When the building of a "New World Order" began, the road was rough and rugged. Europeans, like Africans, had equal shares of work. However some "whites" like "blacks" did not like to work. In order to instill fear and order they were whipped, white and black alike. There was equality, there was unity, and there was one. "Familiarity breeds contempt --- and children"

The kids of the following generations began to dislike the "racial unity" that was being promoted by their parents. So what they did is begin to separate themselves by color. The children, not telling their parents, began to make a different language that was unlike the mother language, slang. As they grew up, the kids' slang became the new language of the new generation. The "blacks" had their own slang and the whites had their own slang.

Because America was a white man's country, he invented "nigger." The characteristics of a nigger has always present in nature. A person of color, who is ignorant, lacks education, formal language, a slave, and is socioeconomically disadvantaged would be considered a nigger. Finding a nigger wasn't the hard part, making it a reality was. Who in this world doesn't have color? If you can find a clear person, set this on fire! Who in this world isn't ignorant to some extent? Show me a know-it-all and I'll show you a God. Yeah, yeah, yeah Bill Gates, Steve Jobs and Oprah have a lot of money, but who's giving it to them? Who in this world doesn't lack education? If you get a Doctorate at Harvard does that mean you're a genius? (Einstein hated school.) Slavery is a mind state, there are people who can physically come and go as they please and they still feel subjugated. So if my "logic" serves me correct, **EVERYONE IS A NIGGER, BUT IF EVERYONE'S A NIGGER, THEN THAT WOULD MEAN.... OH SHIT! I PROBABLY SHOULDN'T HAVE READ THIS FAR... DAMN!**

As stated earlier, in order for something to be a reality, it has to have a name. The name, describes the fantasy so well that it begins to be accepted. But the word has to divide and conquer not unite and liberate. So the word being used has to represent everyone, but we have to teach it to be used one way. This way, the word will always keep its illusion interruption. Oh I got it... "Nigger!"

White kids began using this word toward black kids in the south and then it spread like wildfire. Black kids, having their own language, didn't know what nigger meant so they ignored it. When nigger was only used by white people, it had more meaning because only they knew what it meant. So the word was only used for "black people" because it pertained to everybody but it was funny to call someone in particular a certain name. The problem arose when the word began to get used too much and black people never understood what it meant. Naturally, the body began to reject it and then "black people" began to get "offended." "Curiosity killed the cat."

Nigger then became taboo for white people because they overused it. So the parents who were offended by this word began to teach their kids to get offended. Kids, doing what they are told, adapted to the illusion interruption of getting angry at the word nigger. Not knowing why, when "black kids" heard the word nigger, they told "white kids" "My parents said don't call me nigger, nigger." The white kid, being taught by their parents to call "black kids" nigger, becomes confused. The white kid says "Well my parents said that you're a nigger, so that means you're a nigger!"

What you have is two kids fighting an unsolved battle of the parents. Both of these kids are consumed entirely by illusion interruption. The only niggers here are the kids. A child will die to protect their caregiver because they've been taught to do so. So basically you have here is nothing more than a family feud.

From a comedic standpoint, minstrel shows were used to make niggas look bad. These shows were portrayed by niggas to make fun of other niggas. Ironically, niggas weren't allowed to act during this time so it wasn't actually niggas who looked bad, it was niggas who made niggas look bad. Niggas put on make-up and began to portray niggas in the 1800s. Stereotypes of how niggas acted made niggas laugh. They also used minstrel shows as a means to convince Woodrow Wilson to believe that the Ku Klux Klan was the "Justice League" to protect niggas from niggas. This nigga believes it, the Ku Klux Klan is reformed and they're back on their rampage of killing niggas, freedmen and carpet-baggers alike, but they only showed freedmen being lynched, not carpet-baggers because that would destroy the illusion.

So they'd show niggas being lynched but they refused to show the lynching of Leo Frank. They'd show niggas getting bit by dogs, but they wouldn't focus the camera on "nigger-lovers" that were with them. They'd show Marvin Gaye sing "What's Going On?" but not Bob Dylan singing "Blowin' in the Wind." So the depiction that niggas were only "black" scarred the psyche of niggas and made them believe that they were the only niggas. Them and only them.

"People always clap for the wrong things."

So comedians began to use nigga like the bread and butter for their routines. The only nigga that held power like no other was Richard Pryor. When he said nigga, there was a cadence in his voice that made the word sound poetic, he was actually one of the first niggas who made nigga cool. So nigga was no longer that disparaging, because his use of the word nigga held no color boundary no religion boundary no sex boundary no boundary at all. But when he went to Africa and said that he didn't see niggas there, and said that he would no longer say nigga, he split the word again. The word then became racially charged again.

Niggas claim they hate niggas but love black people. That can't be true because "black" people don't exist, niggas exist because niggas are everybody. Niggas steal pensions, niggas steal cars, niggas break into your house, niggas declare war, and niggas kill. Niggas also fight for the rights of those pension workers, niggas find the niggas that steal cars, niggas made ADT, niggas went to Camp David, and niggas give life. So tell me who's really the nigger, racist? Because I didn't see a "black man" get four gold-medals in Berlin, I saw a nigga. I didn't see a "black man" regretting his claims about white devils when he went to North Africa and seen that the main revolutionaries were "white." I saw a nigga. I didn't see a "black person" get shot in Dallas in a motorcade that supported Civil Rights, I saw a nigga. What black people do you love? Because I love none, I love niggas.

Niggas pride themselves on being "black," but will do the same "nigger" shit they accuse of their people. They do the same exploitation that they accuse the "niggers" they hate, they commit the same offences as "niggers" but yet they hate to be called "niggers" but then they love "black people?"

"Ain't No Love in The Heart of the City."

If it wasn't for the use of the word nigger by whites, then there would've never been a nigga. When niggas started saying "nigga," it was used satirically against niggas. Niggas got so used to saying to "nigger," they no longer noticed. But niggas started saying it so much that they began to believe that they were the only ones who said it. So when niggas heard other niggas saying nigga, it aggravated the first niggas. So what niggas decided to do was create a new word in place of nigga without telling niggas. So niggas stopped calling niggas "niggas" and decided to call them "black." "Satisfaction brought em back."

No longer was a nigga a nigga, a nigga was now black. But because niggas was conflicted with illusion interruption, they began to stop saying nigga and started calling each other "black man." The nigga who made nigger, now making niggas stop saying nigga, started calling niggas nigger again. The new nigga was the "Proud Black Man," that was the thing to be. Marcus Garvey, Langston Hughes, James Baldwin, Martin Luther King Jr., Duke Ellington, Madame C.J. Walker, Harriet Tubman, Malcolm X, Huey P. Newton., John Carlos and Tommie Smith. "Black is beautiful, Black Power, Black Panthers, Black Nationalism." You think you know your history? Prove it.

Who is John Brown? And what was his relationship to Harriet Tubman? Did James Baldwin believe he was "black?" Susan B. Anthony helped Frederick Douglass with the passing of the 15th Amendment, but did Frederick Douglass help Susan with the Suffrage? Who taught Frederick Douglass how to read? What did Duke Ellington classify his music as? Who did Martin Luther King Jr. get his teachings from? Why did Michael King name Michael King Jr. after the man who started the Protestant Reformation? Why was Spain forced to find another route to Asia? Why was Madame C.J. Walkers' hair care product so important? A lot of "brothers" use "Uncle Tom" as a racial epithet, then feel free to tell me why this book was banned in Russia as well as the U.S.? Was Malcolm X more effective when he was a "Black Muslim" or when he embraced the brotherhood of all men? If Lenin had not been born would the Black Panthers have been created? John Carlos and Tommie Smith did what? "Ya'll some stupid niggas stuck in illusion interruption."

If you can answer any of these questions without giving an answer that transcends race, then please feel free to walk away, but if you're still here then you realize that there is no such thing as "black" or "white." "White" is the color of this paper, "black" is the color of this ink. I can't write this paper without black ink, and I can't put black ink on black paper. I couldn't put white ink on white paper, so what does that tell you? We're all niggers. "If everyone was a nigger, would anyone be a nigga?"

"I believe in the brotherhood of man, all men, but I don't believe in brotherhood with anybody who doesn't want brotherhood with me. I believe in treating people right, but I'm not going to waste my time trying to treat somebody right who doesn't know how to return the treatment."

Jesse Owens defamed the 1968 Olympics, I can see why... The "black man" is the Sophists to Plato's Philosophy, the Cointelpro to the Black Panthers, the bullet to Biggie and Tupac, the P.A.T.R.I.O.T. act. The "black man" is the unrequited love that holds on to the past of their "ancestors" and uses that as a fucking excuse for every personal failure. 2009 failures are blamed on 1879 successes. The "black man" is the biggest threat to niggas. The "black man" is the racist. "This Can't Be Life."

"In the past, yes, I have made sweeping indictments of all white people. I will never be guilty of that again — as I know now that some white people are truly sincere, that some truly are capable of being brotherly toward a black man."

I probably don't know my "history" but you don't know yours either. You think I'm lying, tell a "black man" that he's going back to Africa tomorrow. He'll break the fuck down and cry. Niggas hate "black people" because they won't admit they're human, they won't admit they're sinners, they won't admit they're niggers, they won't admit they're racist. There is no "culture" more emulated and let me repeat in bold italics on caps lock for emphasis, ***THERE IS NO "CULTURE" MORE EMULATED, MORE IMITATED, MORE EMBRACED,***

***MORE ACCEPTED, MORE ENTICING, AND MORE LOVED THAN** "BLACK CULTURE." **EVERYONE SEEMS TO SEE THIS BUT THE FUCKING** "BLACK CULTURE." **NIGGAS DIED FOR WHAT NIGGAS HAVE NOW, AND WHAT DO NIGGAS DO WITH IT.** "HERE, I DON'T WANNA BE A NIGGA I WANNA BE BLACK, NIIGGAS MAKE US LOOK BAD NIGGAS WERE SLAVES NIGGAS WERE TOLD TO GO TO THE BACK OF THE BUS, I COULD NEVER BE A NIGGER, I COULD NEVER BE A SLAVE, FUCK NIGGERS"*

What the fuck is "black?" Fuck "black!" Fuck "white!" Being "black" now is equivalent to being "white" in the 20s (or even now for that matter). Open disrespect for **every** race but a perverted narcissism for "their own." Ironically this narcissism breeds, not love but twice as much hate for those who display a nigga characteristic. "Blacks" feel that they should be treated better for something that some of them never had to go through. They give this anecdote about "Kings and Queens of Africa" and proud to be African, but when they actually see Africans they laugh and mock the culture they claim to love. Well fuck being "black," "African-American," "colored," "pick ninny," "Negro," or anything else that divides. I'd rather be the Uncle Tom nigga that treats everyone the same. One thing I could say about Tom, he wasn't a snitch. "Black people" will worship Abraham Lincoln, but neglect to acknowledge the people who provoked him to make his decision.

"You may dispose of me very easily. I am nearly disposed of now. But this question is still to be settled, this Negro question, I mean; the end of that is not yet."

"Is *man* ever a creature to be trusted with wholly irresponsible power? And does not the slave system, by denying the slave all legal right of testimony, make every individual owner an irresponsible despot? Can anybody fall to make the inference what the practical result will be?"

"If I could save the Union without freeing any slave I would do it; and if I could save it by freeing some and leaving others alone I would also do that. What I do about slavery, and the colored race, I do because I believe it helps to save the Union."

Now I may not know history, but I understand the present and that's all I need to influence the future.

If you asked "white people" for all the reasons why they can't say nigger you'll hear: Slavery, being the number one reason, is why "white" people can't say "nigger." Racism is another reason why the "white man" can't say "nigger." Lynching is one more reason that the "white man" can't say nigger. Ummm....Rosa Parks is another reason. The assassination of Malcolm X, Martin Luther King Jr, and Huey P. Newton, more reasons. The "distribution" of "AIDS" and "crack" are more reasons. Wait there's more! The unsolved deaths of Tupac Shakur **and** Biggie Smalls are two more reasons. The attempt to impeach Bill Clinton is another reason, followed by 8 years of Bush. What you have here is the reasons why "white people" can't say "nigger." What you also have is the history of what it means to be "White-American." Wait! How could I forget the most obvious answer? "Because they're not black." Ask this same "white person" if they're racist, they'll sincerely say… "No." The past will always conflict with the present, thus influencing the future… "Illusion interruption."

I asked a nigga why he doesn't say "nigga." He told me because "Niggas will fuck him up." I asked him if he ever got beaten up before, he said yes. I asked him did he say "nigga" to get beat up, he said no. "Excuses are like assholes, everyone's got them and" they'll shit on you if you give them the chance.

The same "Slavery" that was forced upon "blacks" is the same "slavery" that is forced upon **everybody** but niggas don't see it that way…

The Japanese were detained in concentration camps during World War II, were niggas marching then? When Emmet Till was slaughtered, were niggas marching then? But when someone sits down on a bus, it makes all the difference? "Politics as Usual."

This same "Mother of Modern Day Civil Rights" sues "her own" for using her name on a song. I love my people. Well "What's love got to do with it?"

One thing I love about niggas, they say whatever they want. Racists keep their thoughts to themselves, and for good reason. Niggas will fuck them up if they ever said what they felt. Racists use niggas to say what they can't say. A racist won't say "nigga," but a nigga will say it. You ask a nigga if they're a nigga, they'll say "Yes!" Ask a racist if they're racist they'll say "No!" Everyone wants to be a nigga, but no one wants to be a racist, something's gotta give.

"Daddy when I grow up I'm gonna be a basketball player!"

"Jonathan! Only niggers do that, be a lawyer I hear they make good money."

"But Dad I'm really good and—"

"Now I don't care about these fantasies and dreams that you have! You have to be realistic, now I tried to play basketball and they told me I couldn't because I wasn't good enough and they'll tell you the same thing. I'm only doing this because I love you"

"Okay Dad."

"Ma, when I grow up I'm gonna be the next President!"

"Now you know they'll never let a black man be the President of this country, be a basketball player I hear they make good money!"

"But Ma I've been studying law and politics and---"

"Listen, I understand that you have these dreams and that's a good thing to aspire to, but you have to stay grounded. They'll never allow you to become the President, when I was a kid they wouldn't even let us eat in their diners so what makes you think times have changed? Look I love you and I'm doing what's in your best interest."

"Yes Ma."

This is the type of shit that niggas had to hear from racists. Ask these parents are they racist and they'll sincerely say "No."

The past will always conflict with the present, thus influencing the future. Illusion Interruption.

It was something else racist parents told their kids. I can't remember, oh wait now I do.

"Because you're black."

Racist"
l"

Revolution is the product of hate, humility and awareness. Revolution is a sudden, radical and complete change of an established system. Revolution is the essential factor in human evolution, because revolution is so sudden and radical that it forces people to adapt quickly. This adaptation causes people to modify themselves in order to accommodate change. Revolution determines whether a system continues or ceases. Hatred, humility, and awareness are the factors of this equation. Humility is the virtue that places people at the bottom; at the bottom, people become aware of their environment because they see the foundation of society. All things have a foundation, without a foundation there is no existence. This reality causes the humble to become bitter. This bitterness soon becomes hatred, and their antipathy becomes motivation towards change. Revolutions are so sudden that they become unpretentious. This unpretentiousness reflects the entity that starts it; humility. There is no affection in revolution, there is only hate. Revolution takes no prisoners, because revolution has no love. This extreme emotion brings extreme change; through this extreme change revolution is born.

Rebellion is the product of love, pride and ignorance. Rebellions are usually an instance of unsuccessful defiance or resistance against an established system. Rebellion is the obligation to the fool; those who believe that their instances of defiance cause change in society are ignorant. Their love for their self-image taints their psyche. The adulteration of their psyche makes them ignorant. They take pride in their love of ignorance; this bliss is the reason why rebels fail. Rebels are only concerned with their self-image. They don't want to overthrow society; they want to be admired by it. Their egos become their downfall, because they don't know who they're fighting. Rebels believe that there enemy can be destroyed with instances of rebellion. These instances lead to the death of rebels, because the only enemy that the rebel has is themselves.

Rebels don't evoke revolution, they only prolong it. Rebellion are based on emotions, these emotions make rebels inept. Their ineptness makes them "rebels without causes." Rebels' actions are usually pretentious, they have to conjure up an audience or they feel inadequate. Their inadequacy is their downfall, because their egos aren't fed by others. Rebels soon lose sight on what they were originally fighting and end up only fighting themselves. This internal battle postpones revolution. Their ego allows the rebel to believe that revolution can be put off until they feel like doing it. Their volatile attitude is the reason why the rebel only shows instances of resistance. Their ego prevents them from seeing the real world, because they're in a fantasy one. This is what separates the revolutionary from the rebel, the "social-messiah" from the "social-martyr," the men from the mice.

Our defining moments are those in which we cannot control. This is what separates mice from men. While mice avoid danger by hiding in cracks and corners, men stand strong in the face of adversity with forbearance and courage. Man has accepted his fear and placed it on his forehead for all to see. This display of humbleness allows man to become stronger than ever. With their weakness being displayed, it makes harder for their enemies to attack them because man has accepted their faults. The acceptance of their flaws has turned their worst enemy into their closest ally. Courage is not an act of pride; it is an act of humility. The realization of our personal flaws evolves into the realization of everyone else's. This enlightenment can only be achieved through humility. Humility is the virtue that places us below the standard of human cognition. This sub-standard cognition makes us question what is wrong with ourselves. Curiosity causes us to venture for an answer; in our venture we understand the foundation of our ailment. We become aware of our own ailment, and realize that our ailment is a reflection of society's ailments. Humility looks at the foundation of the proud and can recognize what the proud can't; imperfection.

The beauty of humility is so simple, it perplexes the mind. The perplexity of humility understands the most complicated situations, with the most effortless applications. Humility softens the heart and hardens the mind; when we are humble, we don't feel as much because we hate everything, but we do think clearer. Humility is able to look at both sides of situation impartially. This impartiality makes Humility more reasonable and logical; because it hates both sides it can't pick favorites. Favoritism is the foundation to all inequality and injustice, but because this feat doesn't exist in the humble they are able to see things for what they are. Humility can look at the foundation of the proud, and know at any given moment that they can destroy their foundation. The awareness of the humble makes them cynical towards society. The humble find it hard to understand why the proud are so pretentious. To the humble, the proud have nothing to be proud of. They have this advantage over their counterpart, but won't expose it because their humility has not told them to do so; yet. This feat is what makes the humble more dangerous than the proud.

Humility will keeps us alive, but pride will kill slowly and painfully. Pride destroys our sanity and makes blind to the obvious; pride is the entity that hardens heart and softens the mind. With pride, we no longer think, we only feel. Pride is a cognition based on emotion not logic. When our pride takes over, we feel we're doing what's best, but this is only what we feel. In actuality, we neglect logic and reasoning with our feelings, because we're only trying to please ourselves. This blindness takes away from the reality and causes the blind to live in a parallel universe commonly known as fantasy. Now it is understood that self-indulgence is the foundation of psychopaths. Society has instilled self- indulgence within our lifestyle, so inadvertently they have instilled us with psychopathic behavior. Psychopathic behavior is usually unacceptable, but if psychopathic behavior becomes accepted, then it becomes *niggel*. The normalcy of psychopathic behavior becomes standard. Those who aren't self-indulgent are not psychopaths, those who aren't psychopaths aren't *niggers*. Consequently, those who aren't *racist* aren't psychopaths; those who aren't psychopaths aren't self indulgent. This threatens the psyche of the modest and the humble, because they are not the paradigm of self- indulgence; they are the psychopath.

This separates the "social-messiah" from the "social-martyr." The social-martyr is the proud, and the social- messiah is the humble. The martyr fights the battles, while the humble fights the wars. The social- martyr is concerned with small triumphs because it feeds their big egos.

The social- messiah isn't concerned with winning. They know that a revolution has no winners; there is only improvement or stagnation. The social- messiah knows that the only difference between winning and losing is the way the social-martyr looks at it. Defining moments is the "iron curtain" that defines the social- messiah and the social-martyr. The social- martyr tries to control definitive moments with narcissism. Their narcissism entraps the social- martyr within their own consciousness. They are unable to see the big picture because they're only focused on their own painting. Their painting is one of grandeur and genteel. It is carefully crafted; no smudges, no blights, no dispositions, to them their picture is perfect. They see nothing wrong with the world, because they see nothing with their picture. The social- martyr only becomes defiant if something stains their "perfect picture." This is when you see the social- martyr become rebellious; because their picture is destroyed they want to destroy everyone else's. The social- martyr is willing to die for their painting, making them slaves to their own narcissism. As long as the social- martyrs' picture remains untainted, then the social- martyr remains silent.

The social- messiah realizes that defining moments are beyond the control of their free will. The social- messiahs even acknowledge that their own free will is limited due to the infringement of society. This early disposition has made their picture a grand hall. Their hall is desecrated with the reality that the world is bigger than them. Their existence is not separate from the world; it is a part of it. They realize that the world doesn't change on its own, people change it; some for the better, some for the worse, whatever the case it still changes. Their picture is messy, grimy, gritty, and raw. There is no organization in their picture, because there is no organization in their hall. There is no organization in the hall, because there is no organization in existence. The social- messiahs' picture is unlike the social- martyrs'; whereas the social- messiahs' picture is real; the social- martyrs' picture is fantasy.

The social- messiah has seen their painting damaged by seeing the desecration of the grand hall. Their destroyed proportion causes them to resent their own existence. In their resentment they see their own existence destroyed by the infringement of society. They have been forsaken by society, so they have forsaken society. Their bitterness grows as they begin to question their existence. As they question their existence, they question the existence of the world. This reflection causes resentment, resentment and bitterness makes the ultimate emotion; hate. Through this hatred, they understand that the only way to have a better world is to make a better world. This is when the social- messiah accepts revolution as their savior and seeks refuge in it.

Revolution does not have a perspective, it has a definitive property. This property is hatred; revolutions only occur when the established system is no longer accepted. This reaction breeds hate and invokes change. People who say that they hate the establishment but abide by it are liars. The social- martyrs are the biggest liars; they will never fight against the system, because they love it. The only way a martyr will fight the system; is when the system destroys the martyrs' "picture." This interference threatens their ego and the social- martyr becomes defensive. Although, the social- martyr is angry, their anger is not strong enough to revolutionize the system, but it is only weak enough to rebel against it. They know that they cannot rebel by themselves, so they become demagogues. In their demagoguery, their egos promise what their actions can't; revolution. These promises persuade people to follow, for a cause that they are unaware with. Those who follow reflect those who lead; the unawareness of the follower is a reflection of the unawareness of the leader.

Social- martyrs can only persuade social- martyrs, because they're unified through self- indulgence. When this self- indulgence is amplified, it becomes a society within society. This sub- society reflects the establishment, but accommodates the social- martyrs more than their original society did. The martyrs' egos have tricked their consciousness, making them believe that they have started a revolution. In reality, they have only rebelled against the establishment making the establishment stronger than before. The ignorance of the martyr entraps their reality into a labyrinth of fantasy. The fantasy is so intricate, that the martyr ends up fighting the same battles repeatedly, but because their ego holds them captive the same battles look different. This déjà vu drives the social- martyr insane; this insanity leads to the destruction of the social- martyr. The only enemy that the social- martyr has is themselves.

The flapper movement of the 1920's is a clear example of the rebel. During the 1920s, a lot was changing. World War I had just ended, blacks migrated to the north in hopes to get better jobs; the Woman's Suffrage movement allowed women to have the right to vote, and jazz was the new music that defined this generation, the stock market crashed and the prohibition of liquor was enforced by national legislature. With this rapid change in American culture, it was easy to see that things would not stay the same. Blacks were now becoming a part of mainstream America, with the help of jazz. Fortunately, jazz didn't only uplift African-Americans it also uplifted women. During the woman's suffrage, something happened; woman across the world not just America was rising against the system of patriarchy that had long been established. With woman now challenging their place in society a lot of conflict rose amidst females in the 1920s. Some woman wanted to continue to keep up society's standard of a woman's role and some wanted to rebel against it; those women who rebelled were called "flappers."

The term "flapper" was first used to describe the form of jazz that was being played during the early 20s. This new age of jazz was seen as dangerous to the conservative population of America because it challenged all traditional values of America. Naturally, every generation defines themselves with war, media, drugs, and economy; the flappers were no different. "Flapper" refers to the action of the bird. As birds flap their wings they elevate above all control and are controlled by their own will. The same action that birds used to fly above the standard gravity, so did the new breed of woman in the 1920s. This breed of woman was free from coercion, from control; this new woman was free. Flappers were the paradigm of the free woman during the 1920s; they wore makeup, drank liquor, had sex promiscuously, smoked, wore high skirts, danced provocatively, and drove cars. These women were free from the system of patriarchy. Flappers normally stood out in stood out in society with their high skirts, bobbed hair, and heavy makeup. They showed obvious disdain for everything traditional, with good reason; everything traditional system was based on the patriarch, men have subjugated women for centuries, and now that women finally had freedom, they wanted to flaunt it as much as possible. They sniffed cocaine and drank openly because they wanted to turn away from the conventional ways of the woman.

Ironically enough, the flapper in all their belligerent behavior remained rebels. They did not revolutionize the way a woman was conceived they only rebelled against it. There were still few women who held high positions of power, there were lots of female actors but not a lot female directors. Although these women were being free, they didn't do anything but rebel. Now more than ever did men believe that their assumption of women were right; in religion and science men were taught that the woman was far less rational and logical than men, they were uncontrollable creatures who were the sole reason for mankind's ostracism from paradise. The flapper did not change this, they only solidified it. Even the flappers' fashion reflected rebellious ways instead of revolutionary ones; they cut their hair in boyish hairstyles, they stopped wearing corsets which emphasized their feminine physique, and they wore hats which were originally made for young boys. The flapper subconsciously showed their love for the patriarch system; they wore bust bodices and new corsets which emphasized a boyish look rather than a feminine one. Even the flapper's bras were now made to take away from the breast area, making them look virtually like men. Although society forsakes the flapper, the flapper has not done the same, because they suppressed their femininity to look like boys. Although the flapper externally showed disdain for the patriarch, they subconsciously only showed just how much they loved the patriarch by dressing and acting like men. The flapper was indeed a popular movement, but unfortunately it was not a lasting one; with the Great Depression, society called for traditional revival; woman could not get the jobs afforded to men at this time and once again the flapper had to be subjugated back to where they first rebelled against; under a man's arm.

The social- messiah is the true revolutionary. The social-messiahs are the ultimate enemy of the establishment. Society is disgusted by their existence, so it is usually society that destroys them. The social-messiahs awaken the social-martyr from their self-indulgent fantasies. The social-martyr loves their ignorance, and will not allow anyone to come between them and their happiness. The social-messiah knows this and they capitalize on it. This is when the bittersweet relationship of the social-messiah and the social-martyr begins. The social-messiah understands the psyche of the social-martyr, better than they understand themselves. Their disdain for the social-martyr causes them to learn about them in ways that they don't understand. In their illumination, they discover that the foundation of the martyr is pride. They have seen the covenant between the martyr and its pride. They understand the frailty of the martyrs, and won't expose their weaknesses, not unless they have to.

The social-messiah knows how the martyr functions; this gives the messiah the advantage. The messiah feeds the egos of the martyr with their humility for the sake of revolution. They have no problem in allowing the martyr to believe that they're fighting the war. The messiah knows that the martyrs' psyche will only limit them to be satisfied with the battles, because the martyrs' ego needs instant satisfaction. The martyrs' egos haven't allowed them to grasp the bigger picture. Because the martyr is essentially fighting for themselves they are fighting for nothing, however because the messiah knows this, the martyr will be used to fight for everything. Martyrs are willing to die for their own cause, so it is imperative that the messiah convinces the martyr that the bigger picture is the one their fighting for. This bittersweet relationship has evolved into something greater; revolution. Social-messiahs once despised the psyche of the martyr, but because the messiah understands the martyr, they can effectively use them as chess pieces. The messiah would rather the martyr die for a bigger purpose besides the fulfillment of their own egos.

Mary Wollstonecraft was a true revolutionary to the feminists' movement. She was a pioneer on what conflict between what a woman's role should be. Her book "Vindication on the Rights of Woman" revolutionized contemporary thought in 18th century. In this book Wollstonecraft showed how religion and politics were **concepts** both used to enslave and subjugate the minds of women in the 18th century. Her book was made with the intention to deliver woman from the control of men's grasp within the generation. Her book was vengeance towards Charles Maurice de Talleyrand-Périgord's comment to the French National Assembly stating that women only deserved a domestic education. This book was to show society just how many double-standards were acceptable between men and women.

Woman in the 18th century were lower than slaves. Slaves were constantly debated on; the debate was whether having slaves was moral or immoral. Slaves were not even considered people at this time, they were considered property. Ironically enough there was still question whether slavery was ethical. Meanwhile, woman's rights were not debated upon because they were not even conceivable at that time. There was no doubt what a woman's place was in the 18th century. They had specific jobs that were designated only for them and no woman could debate about this system, because the system was not designed with women in mind. A revolution was in dire need, because women were not a part of society because society held disdain for them.

Mary Wollstonecraft became the ultimate revolutionary in writing this book. She did what no one thought was possible; not only challenge a woman's place in society but also challenge a man's logic and reasoning. Wollstonecraft says:

Men, in general, seem to employ their reason to justify prejudices, which they have imbibed, they cannot trace how, rather than to root them out. The mind must be strong that resolutely forms its own principles; for a kind of intellectual cowardice prevails which makes many men shrink from the task, or only do it by halves. Yet the imperfect conclusions thus drawn, are frequently very plausible, because they are built on partial experience, on just, though narrow, views.

This quote illustrated the partisan and bias control of society. Wollstonecraft shows that men often have faulty logic and reason because they only employ their partial reasoning and discount women. In doing this, they only have partial logic because they discounted the other half necessary to make logical decisions. Wollstonecraft says that they are able to do these things and justify it with their logic, but if their logic is partial then so is their justice. She says that men hide behind their faulty logic to make things seem justifiable and reasonable.

In another explanation she says:

Rousseau became enamored of solitude, and, being at the same time an optimist, he labors with uncommon eloquence to prove that man was naturally a solitary animal. Misled by his respect for the goodness of God, who certainly—for what man of sense and feeling can doubt it!— gave life only to communicate happiness, he considers evil as positive, and the work of man; not aware that he was exalting one attribute at the expense of another, equally necessary to divine perfection.

This quote shows just Rousseau's in depth analysis of man as a solitary animal. Wollstonecraft only uses his belief as satire to show just how partisan a man's logic is. She says that even men misconstrue their belief in God when discounting women; men believed that God was good and created everything in his image, and then certainly woman had to be made in the image of goodness considering that they were made in the image of God. Once again, Wollstonecraft shows how man's partial logic fails their reasoning; if God is good and created everything then that would make woman god as well as men, but because men often discount that testimony they often discount divine perfection. In doing that, man is blaming woman for everything that is wrong with the world not realizing that they are taking their faulty logic out of the equation. This shows just how much the revolutionary mind exposes the mind of the rebel. Men are rebellious against their own logic because their logic is partial. Wollstonecraft book proves it, because she shows how man's attempt to justify prejudice only hinders man's ability to become whole. In this attempt men become the rebel of the 18th century and woman become the revolutionary. It is notable to say that if Wollstonecraft had not written this book then the birth of woman's Suffrage may have not happened when it did. Without Women's Suffrage, the birth of the flapper would have not been successful either. So it is understood that we need both rebels and revolutionaries.

Behind every rebellion there is a revolution, behind every rebel there is a revolutionary, behind every rebellious act there is a revolutionary one. These two concepts are dependant of each other; without martyrs' ignorance, the awareness of the messiah cannot happen, without the martyrs' love for society, the messiah cannot hate society, without the martyrs' pride, the messiah cannot become humble. The reciprocity of obligation causes these two concepts to flourish; this prosperity is what revolutionizes society.

We see the difference between rebellion and revolution, so what is holding us back? The truth is we have all become fascinated with our own paintings. All of us are entrapped within fantasy's labyrinth, and this entrapment is the reason why a revolution has yet to occur. Until all of our paintings are kicked in suddenly, there will be no improvement, there will only be stagnation. Every revolution breeds an antagonist and protagonist; the suffrage brought out the feminists and the flappers.

My revolution was bred in…

For decades, the media and politicians have been successful in bringing important issues to the surface. They have been effective in allowing us to understand the events of this great country. As problems arise, they bring extreme emotion to those watching. This allows the viewer to become captivated by the news. In the viewer's captivation, their minds become sponges, soaking and absorbing everything and anything the media and politicians tell them. Although the media has done an exceptional task with presenting solutions to certain problems, they have often neglected an essential aspect to every problem: the underlying causes which lead to these events.

Emotions can make us logically inept. These initial responses tend to be what the media and politicians facilitate. This illustrates the power of demagogues in society. Their tactics are effective, but views expressed by them are partisan and biased. Their arbitrary views have led to unjust treatment of the media's targets. What's even more disappointing is that demagogues have used tactics so effective, that it has allowed society to adopt the same views. This has allowed society to designate the same "enemies" as the media, because of this, the media and society now have the same enemy. This enemy can now be identified on sight and attacked.

Crack was a catalyst for one of the most vicious epidemics in American history. It was successful in helping destroy impoverished communities across the nation. In addition, crack has allowed politicians and media focus their attacks on a class that has been long undermined. Since its arrival, the media has been effective in its efforts to show the connection between drugs and the communities in which it affects. The depictions that crack have produced a "lost generation" encouraged society to cast them out. While they look at the effects of crack in African-American communities, they often refuse to acknowledge the underlying causes which lead to the abuse of the drug on both sides of the spectrum, the dealer and the user. The same addiction that the drug addict possesses with crack is the same addiction the dealer possesses with money. These two factions were formed in a midst of an epidemic, and pitted this sub-culture against each other. With this friction rapidly occurring in inner-cities, it has internally destroyed the communities and has allowed the media and politicians to make their attacks more effective and potent.

A criminologist named Steven Spritzer describes two types of people discarded by capitalism. "Social junk" and "social dynamite," The "social junk" is the people who are broken by the system. In their dissatisfaction they become mentally ill, drug addicts, and cast-off impoverished seniors; Spritzer describes them as the population who are lonely, with no expectation for a future. Examples of social junk plague the ghettos of America, high school basketball players that have dreams of going to the NBA. For whatever reason, they do not get into the colleges of their choice due to poor grades and SAT scores. They bank so much of their futures on this one dream that when their dreams are shattered; they do not know what to do. Depression soon follows, leading to an array of escapisms that usually include the use of alcohol and/or drugs. War veterans in America are a clear example of this explanation. They have fought for this country to protect democracy, but their gratuitous efforts have been met with neglect. Returning home they expect to have their courageous acts met with appreciation. Instead, they come home only to find out that drugs destroy their neighborhoods. In their dissatisfaction they turn to drugs. Post dramatic stress has made their nerves uneasy, and drugs seem to be the only answer.

America's working class wasn't left out either. Consider the unemployed middle class during the recession of 1981, in a one-year span the unemployment rate rose from 11.3% in 1980 to 13.5% in 1981. What is more disturbing is the unemployment rate of African Americans. With unemployment going from 13.5% in 1980 to 18.5% in 1981, it was not easy for an African American to keep a job in the 80s. With unemployment sweeping African American neighborhoods, working class mothers and fathers found it harder than ever to provide for their families. When families that could once provide, lose their jobs where does that leave them?

The other population discarded by capitalism is the "social dynamite". Spritzer elaborates on this population stating –

Social dynamite are those who pose an actual or potential political change, they are the population, which threatens to explode: the impoverished low-wage working class and unemployed youth have fallen below the statistical radar, but whose spirits are not broken and whose expectations for a decent life and social inclusion are dangerously alive and well. They are the class that suffers from "relative deprivation." Their poverty is made all the more unjust because it has experienced in contrast to the spectacle of opulence and the myths of social mobility and opportunity. Controlling them requires both a defensive policy of containment and an aggressive policy of direct attack and active destabilization. They are contained and crushed, confined to the ghetto, demoralized and pilloried in warehouse public schools, demonized by a lurid media, sent to prison, and at times dispatched by lethal injection or police bullets. This is the class – or more accurately the caste, because they are increasingly people of color – which must be undermined, divided, intimidated, attacked, discredited, and ultimately kept in check.

The "social dynamite" is the inner city drug dealer. A large number of drug dealers are usually from broken homes; they experience some of the worst living and learning conditions that America has to offer. Poor health, broken homes and poor education forces them into a corner of degeneracy. They have seen their parent's abuse alcohol and drugs, they have been exposed to domestic violence at early ages, and they have sat in the back of class wanting to learn but due to poorly equipped inner city schools they have lacked the essential knowledge which allows them to become productive members of society. There have been countless times in which they have come home and watched the endless onslaught of slander against their people and culture. They have watched friends and family be carried off to jail or come home in caskets.

Watching television, the "social dynamite" is shown images of happiness. In an effort to replicate such happiness, they turn to drug dealing. This is not because this is their first option but it is usually their last and only option. Lawyers, bankers, and doctors are not common in these neighborhoods, but drug dealers are. This is not to say that people who grow up in poor neighborhoods can't become doctors and lawyers, but it is to say that chances of these events are few and far between. These productive careers are rare in impoverished neighborhoods, because these neighborhoods are poorly nourished in these fields. The "social-dynamite" is not groomed into wealth and education like the children of prominent business owners; instead, they become products of their own environment. Unfortunately, the dealers' environment does not nurture them in a way accepted by society, but only teaches them to achieve goals through familiar means. Most dealers do not come into dealing drugs with the mindset that they will have to kill, rob or destroy. Instead, all they want is what Thomas Jefferson said we have the right to as American citizens, life, liberty, and the pursuit of happiness.

The purpose of this explanation is not to "pardon" drug-dealers for their exploits; instead, to clarify certain circumstances that inner city drug dealers deal with. Drug dealers have undeniably robbed their communities of self-esteem, integrity, and respect. They have killed, robbed, kidnapped, and have been the destructive force in the same communities they claim to take pride in. They attempt to compensate for this destruction by occasionally giving back, but no gifts or amounts of money can equate the loss of lives claimed by their vicious actions. Their destructive actions have compromised the integrity of their original intentions. When they say "I love my people," that can no longer be believed, because their actions have shown otherwise. These "prominent business men" have allowed these events to occur in the name of capitalism. They have not only become products of their environments, but they become a reflection of their society. This illustrates that in the name of "competition" people are willing to destroy everything to become the best, in their cases, their own self-identity. Their application of capitalism commonly reflects the values that society has placed on the concept. What society calls capitalism, drug dealer's calls success. Just like CEO's who believe that they shouldn't be punished for the exploits of their "corporations", drug dealers feel the same way; blame shouldn't be on the dealer, it should be on the user. That's what crack was in the 80's, a Limited Liability Corporation.

When certain benefits are taken from the "social dynamite," it leaves them with very few options causing them to make choices out of desperation and not freedom. Being deprived of essential resources necessary to succeed, makes the dealer animalistic, because society has left them with no other choice. Drug-dealers like most American citizens just want to have nice houses, nice cars, and happy families. That is the "American Dream," to come from the abyss of despair and rise to the pedestal of prosperity, through hard work and determination. Unlike, the "social junk" they will not allow their parents curse to become their own. They are not given the same tools to succeed so they use what they know to get what they want. Like anyone who is driven by profit, the ends justify the means. Some dealers see the robberies, homicides, and hardships they encounter as obstacles necessary to make them the best. The same "social-Darwinism" that is promoted amongst young interns competing for a job at a major corporation is the same attitude present in drug dealers. They have adopted the "American Dream" and manipulated it to their environment. This has made them successes in their neighborhoods. Unfortunately, their "success" is not accepted by society. Society's disdain for their lifestyle discredits any attempts made by the "social dynamite" to be accepted. While the "social dynamite" becomes misfits in society, they must now develop their own society that glorifies their lifestyles and experiences.

Although crack is a derivative of cocaine and has most of the same long-term effects as the parent drug, lawmaker feel that because crack is more "addictive" and has been commonly linked to more violent crimes such as homicide and robbery, it justifies the double-standard which allows harsher punishment. Cocaine is seen as a separate entity from crack, with good reason. Although cocaine is addictive and prohibited, it still does not compare to crack. Cocaine does not have the track record of leading to high homicide rates, infant mortality, and high incarcerations. Cocaine was popular for being known as a recreational drug for rich people. Stephen King, Sherlock Holmes, Robert Louis Stevenson, Grover Cleveland, and Ulysses Grant are just some of the names that have been known to use the drug. Whitney Houston was asked during an interview with Diane Sawyer if she ever used crack, and replied, "First of all, let's get one thing straight. Crack is cheap. I make too much money to ever smoke crack. Let's get that straight. Okay? We don't do crack. We don't do that. Crack is wack." Houston seemed to see difference in the drugs, although she was known for using drugs, she was highly offended to be accused of using crack. Her reason for being offended by the assumption was not only because crack was bad, but because crack was known for being a cheap drug. Houston's interview showed an inconvenient truth about crack. Diane Sawyers' assumption about Houston's use of crack was backed by a conventional belief. The belief was that crack is a popular drug amongst people of color because it's cheap.

Cocaine and crack definitely have differences. Crack's freebase has an initially powerful hit, which makes it more addictive. Cocaine is addictive but lacks that power in the first hit, making the craving for the drug controllable. Another difference in the two drugs was the price. The average price for a gram of cocaine during the early 80s was about $300, whereas crack could go for as cheap as $5 a vial. With the differences being surfaced, it is becoming more transparent to see who the preferred user is. The average African- American couldn't afford a gram of cocaine; however they can afford a vial of crack. Although crack is undoubtedly cheap, cocaine is a status drug, making the user feel not only euphoric from the side effect of the drug, but also from knowing that some influential people have once used the drug. Like Whitney Houston pointed out to Diane Sawyer "We make too much money to smoke crack. We don't do that." Well if crack is hamburger helper, then cocaine must be filet mignon to Whitney Houston, and whoever the "we" she referred to is.

.The double standard does not only apply to the drug, but also to punishment. "To be successful against a mass market, mass arrests are required." says Chief Clarence Dickson. Reagan must have been thinking the same thing, because in 1986, America would now enact some of the harshest laws on drugs since the era of bootlegging and prohibition. The Anti – Drug Abuse Act of 1986, made mandatory sentencing the conventional consensus amongst lawmakers. A person who carried only had 5 grams of crack was given the same amount of time as someone who possessed 500 grams of cocaine. Although, the quantity of cocaine is larger, the potency of crack was considered twice as addictive as cocaine, making these harsh laws "fair." During the late 80s crack was becoming the drug of the new generation. Now, because more blacks were being prosecuted more frequently for crack than any other ethnicity, the government found their target, the African American community. The federal prison rates, according to a 1994 source, say that 90% of the federal crack charges belonged to African Americans, whereas only 3.5% belonged to whites.

With all of these African-Americans being locked up, one should ask, how is the federal government so precise and accurate with their arrest and convictions? America was founded on basic principles. These principles which are stated in The Declaration of Independence says "We hold these truths to be self-evident, that all men are created equal, that they are endowed by their Creator with certain unalienable Rights, that among these are Life, Liberty and the pursuit of Happiness." This is the psyche of American society. All men are created equal with unalienable rights which include life, liberty and pursuit of happiness, but it is noteworthy to consider that the African-American population was not taken into account when America was founded in 1776. Although, the birth of the United States officially happened on July 4th, 1776, the 13th amendment was not ratified until December 6th, 1865, which is eighty-nine years later. The 13th amendment abolished slavery and stated that it was permanent in its effort to keep slavery immoral and illegal. Knowing this fact, it is easy to see that this system was never designed with blacks in mind.

Africans originally came to America as property, cargo, and economic investments; they were seen as animals with no rights. Africans were below the statistical radar. They could not read, they could not vote, they could not teach, they could not learn. The African population was ostracized from the moment they got on slave ships. The African-American population was never made to be catered to; the African population was made to cater. The African-American population was always subject to "taxation without representation." This population was objectified as creatures unworthy of education, reason, and intelligence. This was the population who worked but reaped no benefits, which sweat but did not drink who starved but did not eat who died but did not live. The African-American population was a race of dogs for America's discretion. They were to be dealt with accordingly, nothing more, nothing less.

This population was there, but did not exist. Even after, the 13th amendment was ratified in 1865; it took an additional ninety-nine years for blacks to get the right to vote. It is now understood that the African-American population was ignored since the birth of this country. African-Americans were never represented in Congress, because Congress never felt that African-Americans were worthy of such high positions. Legislature never made laws that favored this particular population because legislature never cared for this population. African-Americans were brought over here for one thing only, to serve and protect. They served this country in the production of cotton, making this country one of the most affluent countries in the world; they fought in the place of the wealthy confederate masters who were too cowardice to fight for their own creeds. This system was never designed with

African-Americans in mind; everything an African-American ever did was always untimely, unwise, and illegal. The American Dream never included Africans. To the power structure, African-Americans didn't exist; only niggers did. This is why everything that African-Americans ever did was met with imprisonment, robbery, and murder. African-Americans are not a part of this system, they are separate; African-Americans were bred for destruction.

For the African-American population that continues to chase the American Dream, you are only chasing a dream that was not made for you. While reading, you may feel offended by the amount of cynicism in this writing, but one thing that can be agreed upon is that being African-American comes with little to no privilege in this country. This system was already designed and the blueprint is the American Dream; this blueprint entails that you go to college, get a job, and have two cars, a house, a wife and two kids. In reality, most African-Americans are poorly educated; because of this they cannot get good jobs. An African-American's job choice is just as meager as the conditions most of them live in. Their poor jobs make the want for a house and a car virtually impossible. This dream is emphasized so much, it is now engraved into our DNA that if you are not a part of the American Dream then you are nothing. This is what the brunt of the African-American population feels like, nothing.

Those who continue to chase this dream in unimaginable odds are those who show phenomenal resilience. They are poorly educated, unemployed, economically disadvantaged and live in the projects, but will refuse to let that hold them down. They know their ailments, and so does the federal government... This is the reason why conviction rates of African-Americans were so high in 1980's. This society has one way of defining success, and that is the American way. If you didn't achieve through their means then you didn't achieve anything. Only a few African-Americans make it through the means of the American way, and society knows this. Sad to say, but if you're not a sports athlete, actor, dancer, rapper, singer, comedian, or politician of any kind then you're doing something wrong in American society. America has always kept track of successful blacks, because there hasn't been a lot. And now thanks to crack, the federal government could pull weeds out the garden with ease.

Most drug dealers always find themselves thinking: "How did I get caught?" What they didn't realize is that they were already bred to destroy themselves. Racial profiling has never been a major issue in mainstream America, because mainstream America knows just like the government knows: if you're not doing it our way, then you must be doing it your way. Unfortunately, the other way is the illegal way. These drug dealers were buying Lamborghinis, Ferraris, BMWs, real estate, jewelry, and expensive clothing. These drug dealers were living a life that most celebrities couldn't even afford in that time. They never asked themselves if their lifestyle was attracting too much attention. A large number of successful drug dealers were not from the suburbs; they were from the projects. They didn't go to Harvard or Yale; they dropped out before the 12th grade. They did not work for Merrill Lynch or Goldman Sachs; they worked for themselves. Their father's weren't CEOs; most of their fathers left before they could ride a bike. All along these drug dealers were setting themselves up for destruction.

Everyone knew that if you weren't an entertainer, sports athlete, or politician in the 80's then you had to be selling drugs. Although this assumption was extremely stereotypical and racist, it was usually correct. If you grew up in the projects, dropped out of high school, didn't have a six-figure salary, how can you afford a Lamborghini? You're not an athlete; you've never been seen on television, then you must be doing something illegal. It's an unfair reality, but it is reality nevertheless. This is why drug dealers were able to be captured one after another. These dealers are flaunting a lifestyle that doesn't match their background, and the whole time the whole world is on pause watching these dealers like an episode of Martin. It becomes so easy for society to point it out, that it becomes comedy to those watching the lives of a project drop-out become a millionaire in under a year, get caught and go to jail for 35 years. You always hear drug dealers say "Somebody snitched on me," but what they neglect to realize is that they snitched on themselves, trying to be accepted by a society that wanted nothing to do with them.

Crack undoubtedly destroyed many cities across America. Whether crack's arrival was intentional or coincidental in communities like Harlem, Bedford-Stuyvesant and Lafayette Park poses a bigger question: Was crack another drug used to define a new generation? Or was it intentionally placed in certain communities for intentional destruction? Every generation since the 1900's has been defined by drugs. Since the 1900's drugs have played a major role in this society. The 1920's and 30's was defined by alcohol and the prohibition era. The 60's and 70's was defined by psychedelics, heroin, marijuana, and cocaine. Finally, in the 80's we have crack cocaine; a new drug to define a new generation. What's most interesting is the role that drugs have had in this country's legacy, but unlike all other drugs, crack is the only drug that can be found in certain communities. In addition, this drug can be linked directly to one race; African Americans. This feat has allowed actions taken by politicians to become necessary. When crime rates repeatedly rise in inner-city neighborhoods, but not in suburban ones, it justifies all of the extreme actions assumed by legislature. Why is it all right for a fifteen year-old boy with no criminal record receive a mandatory sentence of five years for a first time offense, whereas, a white male who has abused cocaine be only sentenced to 90 days probation? The cold hearted truth behind this injustice is… Because cocaine is not concentrated in communities with high crime rates, it is not likely that someone who has used cocaine to be necessarily classified as a criminal. On the other hand, crack has a concentrated environment with a concentrated nature, crime. As long as this persists, legislature's action will always be justified.

When looking at economic class it has been sad to see that the economic well-being of a person commonly reflects their skin color. We have seen that the richest drug dealers share the same characteristics as some of the richest CEO's, so what is the real difference? The difference seems to be those who target and those who are being targeted. With today's power structure, it is becoming easier to see what is being seen as acceptable. This power structure along with the help of African-Americans has made this injustice seem fair. All African-Americans aren't involved with drugs, but as long as they keep promoting self-destruction within their own neighborhoods, then nothing will change. It's time that they wake up and acknowledge what is wrong with their society and rise above it. The only way to start a revolution is to become one. Crack has definitely done its damage in America's ghettos. The horrifying part of it is that it's far from over. With high birth and incarceration rates across the United States during this epidemic, what has happened to the guidance of our future? More importantly, what has happened to America's "lost generation?"

Because of the crack epidemic, I am now a....

Since the beginning of mankind, music has played a major role in human society. Music was not only an art form; it was a reflection of human empiricism. Empiricism is the theory of knowledge that derives from experience. Empiricism often discount opinion and hearsay. Instead, empiricists usually rely solely on their own observation as proof for events as oppose to society's doctrine. For those who couldn't illustrate their views through literature or art, music was the savior. Music, like any other form of literature had a purpose. Its purpose was to tell a story in a way that could be understood by anyone. Through this understanding, other cultures are able to learn the traditions and customs of a certain people. Music illuminates the minds of those who listen. This illumination allows the listener to get a different perspective of what's going on in someone else's world.

Much like the jazz and rock-n-roll era in the 1900's music was always something that united people. In addition, music always represented a changing society which depicted the events of a nation. Every time the social climate changed in reality, it was heavily correlated with the artists' creative direction and intuitive ability. There is no originality without inspiration, and with one unforgettable epidemic, this group would not find it hard to be inspired by an era.

Niggaz with Attitude (N.W.A) was one of the most influential rap groups in American history. Their music captivated America and revolutionized hip-hop into what is now called "gangsta rap." Although, their music captured the minds and hearts of their mainstream listeners, their music reflected their society, which was destroyed by the infamous crack epidemic of the 80's. N.W.A. was not only a reflection of their society, but they were the voice of it. During the crack epidemic, America's mainstream made sure that they separated themselves from the black community. Constant attacks on the black community caused the drug dealers who could not be accepted by regular society to make their own. In the creation of their own society N.W.A. was born. Their album "Straight Outta Compton." reflected the views taken by this new society, and became the voice of the lost generation. This generation, which was a product of poverty, drugs, violence, poor education, and police brutality was now unleashed upon the world. It was time for America to see what happens when the social dynamite is ready to explode. As you pop this album into your stereo "You are now about the witness the strength of street knowledge."

"Straight Outta Compton" was N.W.A's first hit single. With 808 drum machines roaring and bass booming in systems everywhere the lost generation unleashed their anger. What's most significant about this group was that N.W.A. was able to express their anger in an acceptable manner. They have seen that selling drugs, becoming gang members, and carrying guns were not productive in America. They have realized that this lifestyle has led to many deaths of their families and loved ones. With this realization the social dynamite has evolved. Where they once believed that they didn't need society, they have now found a way to incorporate their lifestyles through an effective form of expression. N.W.A would prove that free expression is dangerous when given to someone that can use it effectively.

Due to vicious effects of the crack epidemic, the lost generation was displaced in time; with their parents either becoming drug dealers or drug addicts, it was easy to see that this generation was lost. The lost generation was any impoverished child that was born between the years of 1980-1995. Now more than other time in American history, more kids were being displaced from their inner-city homes. The term "babies having babies" was born. During this fifteen-year span, there were overwhelmingly high teenage pregnancy rates in most major cities across America. These mothers were victims of crack abuse and could not provide for their kids. The mothers' crack addiction caused the parents to stray from their responsibilities. In the mothers' distraction, these "crack babies" become malnourished, and psychologically damaged. The Bureau of Child Welfare got involved, taking children away from their homes. This displacement caused these children to develop insecure attachments. These children were destroyed emotionally; they found it hard to trust another person due to their mothers' careless mistakes. Soon, these children became filled with anger, because they felt worthless. Today they have to live with the fact that their mother used crack and that their father was nowhere to be found.

Their displacement in society caused them to stray during their adolescent years. These are the years in which most adolescents use their environments to define themselves, but because most of these kids were displaced from their original homes they become one of two things: either become "social-chameleons" and adapt to their environment using resilience as their weapon or they remain "social-dynamites" and become filled with more anger, waiting for anything to trigger a detonation. The social-chameleons were the kids who were able to adapt to their changing environment. They have withstood being deprived of essential resources afforded to others, they have watched domestic violence, and prostitution, gang violence, and drug abuse plagues their neighborhoods. In most cases, they were moved from their homes and put into group or foster homes. They have attended schools so bad that if the No Child Left Behind act had been enacted back then there would be no public schools in inner-city neighborhoods. These kids have mourned during the coldest winters, and have rejoiced during the hottest summers.

The important thing that separates the social-chameleon from the social- dynamite is the amount of resilience built within this social class. Although, the social chameleon is faced with some of the same disadvantages, they will not allow it to destroy them. These are the kids who raise their brothers and sisters at young ages, help them with their homework and try their best to take care of their family. In the summer, when they are hungry they go to their nearest public school for refuge, receiving free meals from the school's summer food program. These early responsibilities have caused the social- chameleons to mature beyond their years. They are not impressed with the allure of drug dealing, because they have personally seen what happens to those who use it. This realization has caused them to become cynical in cognition but optimistic in action. Although life has been tough for these kids, resilience and optimism keeps them alive. Education is their only escape, so they cling to it like an anchor. Intelligence becomes their foundation, and this allows them to escape the 'hood.

Social-Chameleons are the Cinderella stories of America; in fact the social- chameleon is America. They have come from the worst and transformed it into the best. Unfortunately, instances of the social-chameleon are rare in impoverished neighborhoods. Being a social-chameleon requires a lot of resilience due to the circumstances that they are met with; these are the kids who don't wear nice clothes, because their parents used the school clothes money on drugs. These are the kids who are teased by their peers because they can't afford what their peers' parents can afford. The chameleon is the child that sits in the front of the classroom and learns, while the other kids sit in the back and play; the chameleon wants to be a part of the "popular circle," but the popular circle wants nothing to do with the chameleon because to the social-dynamite the chameleon is not there; they are invisible. Their transparent strength becomes complex to those who don't understand them, causing resentment and dissatisfaction of this class. Due to the dissatisfaction of the social-dynamite class, the social-chameleons are commonly called "sell-outs," and are pushed back into mainstream society. This action has caused the social-chameleon to become successful in most cases. They are no longer accepted by their original society so they now seek refuge in mainstream America.

As for the social-dynamite, their anger has now exploded beyond their control. Their anger reflected their actions, causing them to join gangs, and enjoy it. They have sought refuge in their neighborhoods, and have been warmly accepted with 9mms and "8 Ball." N.W.As' song "Fuck Tha Police" became the social- dynamites national anthem. This song captured the hatred that the social-dynamite held for authority; it explained the racial hatred police had for young black kids in ghettos, assuming that all minorities were involved with something illegal. Ice Cube expresses his frustration stating "they rather see me in the pen/ then me and Lorenzo/ rollin' in a benzo," this line translucently describes the cops disdain for seeing a black youth become successful. Ice Cube also tackles another issue erupting within black communities: the self-loathing of black police officers on the force. Ice Cube delivers this message with the rhyme "don't let it be a black and a white one/ cause he'll slam you down to the street top/ black police showing out for the white cop." This line showed the world just how serious police brutality is. Until then, police actions were seen as justified, but Ice Cube's rhetoric forced others to reevaluate their assumptions. Why are police beating youths? More, importantly, why are black police beating their own people? To answer this question, we must revisit the social- chameleons' displacement from the social- dynamite. Due to the displacement of the social- chameleon by the social- dynamite, the social- chameleon becomes resentful towards the social- dynamite. In this resentment, the social- chameleons must now find revenge. They were now accepted by mainstream America, but were hated by underground America. Their alignment with the mainstream has caused them to destroy their own kind; through this constant friction black on black violence is born.

"Straight Outta Compton" and "Fuck Tha Police" were just one of many songs that defined the lost generation. Their anger, which was suppressed during most of the 80's, was now unleashed all at once. The overwhelming anger leads to more gangs, murders, robberies and deaths. What the lost generation saw as a revolution, everyone else saw as rebellion. A revolution is the change of an original system; all the lost generation did was rebel against it. Although, this wasn't a successful revolution, there was a time in which mainstream America had to turn off radios; because N.W.A. was acquiring a new audience, young white Americans. N.W.A's popularity found its way into the suburbs. This new form of expression, called "gangsta rap," was now known around rich suburbs as "cool." Now more than ever, rich white boys wanted to be "Gangsta Gangsta;" "It's not about a salary/it's all about reality." Their lifestyle of being raised with proper etiquette was no longer fun.

Everybody wanted to sag their pants, with their hats turned backwards. Former heirs to financial dynasties no longer wanted to be accountants, they wanted to sell crack. Lawyers' sons no longer wanted to be doctors or presidents; they wanted to be gang members. This "revolution" scared the CEO's and leaders of the country, because now their sons and daughters wanted to be a part of a lifestyle that they were taught to despise. This fear led to N.W.A being banned on all major radio networks.

Now that mainstream society has received a taste of their own medicine, we see that they do not like it. Being a gangster was a mentality built to destroy the psyche of the average inner-city youth. There was a time when being a crack dealer or a gang member was a disgraceful lifestyle, but the media's glorification of N.W.A. backfired in their faces. The media thought that allowing N.W.A on the air would further the destruction of inner-city neighborhoods; but the media didn't count on N.W.A being accepted by mainstream America. This led to a fast growing urban culture where everyone wants to be a "gangsta." The lost generation has found their voice, and they have done what N.W.A told them to do; "Express Yourself." Unfortunately, they haven't developed the maturity of content within this voice. The lost generation has rebelled against society, but it hasn't revolutionized society; although they have shown what really happens in inner-city neighborhoods, they haven't shown it in a way that makes society want to help. N.W.A has achieved an exceptional task; they have used their voice to captivate a mainstream audience. N.W.A has the power to fight conventional beliefs, but they have yet to use it. Lupe Fiasco says "the ink of a scholar is worth a thousand times more than the blood of a martyr." he seems to understand the real works of a revolutionary. Although, N.W.A was the lost generations' voice, they didn't represent it in the way of a revolutionary; they represented it in the way of a rebel.

The revolutionary fights for others, the rebel fights for himself. The revolutionary achieves a bigger purpose; the rebel achieves their purpose. N.W.A was a powerful group, so powerful that they amplified the crime of violence within their own communities. Out of thirteen songs on the album, only one song is trying to uplift the people of inner-city communities. This is the album that represented the lost generation; there is positivity within impoverished neighborhoods, but this positivity seems to be a fraction of 1/13, which is few and far between. Twelve songs glorify destruction, and only one discusses positive productivity. This was the psyche of the lost generation; although they wanted to be positive producers, they had little to no positive influences. All they seemed to have was the glorification of drugs, the objectification of females, violence, and chaos. This is what defined those who were able to make it out of poor neighborhoods, and those who stayed. When your environment is surrounded by negativity how strong is your resilience? This is what made the by-product of social-chameleons. Although the birth of this class was unintended, it showed that people can strive for change.

Because N.W.A glorified their destruction, and didn't fight against it, they became the ultimate rebels. When the glorification of crime, and violence spread into the suburban communities, it started to become vivid just how dangerous a rebel can be. N.W.As' rebellious behavior influenced the behavior of the preppy kids in communities like Westchester and Beverly Hills. The lost generation was not only the impoverished but now it is also the affluent; rebels affect everyone. This rebellious mentality is what defined the lost generation. They became a generation of complainers, beggars, and sloths; this generation became complacent. Instead of evoking change, the lost generation complained about it. This generation of rebels is awaiting the return of the revolutionary, anyone up to the task? Most of the lost generation's abilities remain dormant, but when these abilities are recognized and utilized effectively, whoa! We may have a revolution! In the words of Public Enemy "Fight the Power!" But for right now, we are all just niggaz with attitudes.

But my nigga mentality reflects...

The birth of America has inspired its citizens to define themselves as a free people. Political freedom is defined by the absence of coercion from another person, especially from sovereignty. Members of a politically free society hold full power over their own lives; public and private. In politically free society, people are able to exchange ideas freely without coercion. Neither society nor government can coerce or infringe a person's liberty. Lord Acton describes political freedom not as means to a higher political end, but as the highest political end. Freedom without coercion is a luxury that is not commonly afforded to humanity. Since the birth of this idea, people have always used political freedom as a means to get what they want. Only a few seem to truly understand the concept of political freedom and liberalism. Instead of using political freedom as fuel for their fire, they have remained true to the unadulterated concept of liberalism. They have not used liberty as a means to a political goal; it was the political goal. With the concept of liberalism being clarified it is easy to see that throughout history it has always been seen by power structures as untimely and unwise.

Martin Luther King Jr. has long been seen as the muckraker for the African- American people. During an era when America was plagued with racial adversity between its white and black citizens, King stood in the face of the oppressor and worked towards liberating the oppressed. Many of his "fellow clergy men" discredited his peaceful and just actions, with the claims that he was a troublemaker and an outsider. To these clergymen, King's actions were "untimely and unwise," they deplored his efforts for bringing liberty to an area that has fought against it for so long. They (clergy-men) believed that the Christian society would eventually allow blacks to be equals, but now was not the time. To understand why these clergymen had such a view is because they were white. Although they were fellows of Christian community, they allowed their racism to cloud their impartial judgment. The clergymen allowed their bias destroy the peaceful actions of civil disobedience by calling it untimely and unwise.

King replied to those critics with one of the most critical letters known to American history. "Letter from a Birmingham Jail" illustrated the importance of liberty in the south. Reasoning with his southern brothers, he questions their logic of liberty. King's reasoning compromises the integrity of their views by showing flaws in their logic. King argues against his clergymen stating-

You deplore the demonstrations taking place in Birmingham. But your statement, I am sorry to say, fails to express a similar concern for the conditions that brought about the demonstrations. I am sure that none of you would want to rest content with the superficial kind of social analysis that deals merely with effects and does not grapple with underlying causes. It is unfortunate that demonstrations are taking place in Birmingham, but it is even more unfortunate that the city's white power structure left the Negro community with no alternative.

This passage illustrates the partisan views of the white power structure in the south. These clergymen have called his actions "untimely and unwise," but King is trying to make the clergymen understand that these "unwise" actions only happened because of unwise causes. The power structure has subjugated the black community. There have been countless times in which blacks were murdered, belittled, and berated. Black people across the south were being lynched, schools and churches were being bombed, and they had to endure being objectified as less than people; they were called "boy" and "son." Finally, when these black communities became fed up with these actions and organize themselves to react, and their actions are called "untimely and unwise." King's purpose is not to negotiate with the clergymen; instead his purpose is to clarify the actions of the black community. When the clergymen have seen the black communities' actions as unjustified, King explains that the causes that lead to the action of blacks have been long undermined and that it is just. King goes on to define liberalism saying that an "Injustice anywhere is a threat to justice everywhere." Liberalism and justice are juxtaposed; you can't have freedom without justice, if you infringe one you compromise another. There is no such thing as freedom without justice. King's struggle to liberate blacks across the south proves that liberty cannot be denied forever; sooner or later people will freedom. King's struggle also reflects the ideas of the enlightenment thinker John Locke. Ironically, John Locke's concept of liberalism is the foreground for the "Declaration of Independence," although the founders of America seemed to use Locke's ideas of liberalism as a foundation, they have neglected the fact that liberalism is afforded to everyone. This is a vivid example of how liberalism is used as a means to a higher political goal and not the highest political goal; the founding fathers built this country on "liberty and justice for all." but they leave out the African- American population. If the forefathers of this great country had interpreted Locke better they would have seen their fatal mistake, making freedom *their* political and not **the** political goal.

John Locke was one of the most influential minds during the "Age of Enlightenment." Locke's ideas have become the epitome of philosophical, political, and psychological thought. Locke can be credited for being one of the revolutionary thinkers behind America: not because he was a part of the revolution, but because his writing influenced the many American revolutionaries. The Declaration of Independence reflected Locke's liberal beliefs. Locke's liberalism is seen as a state of equality, where power and jurisdiction is reciprocal. Locke's idea of liberalism personifies the importance of equality; he believed that no one's power or jurisdiction should extend beyond his or her own length because that would be infringement on someone else's freedom. Locke believed in the equality of men by nature; the obligation of reciprocity allows men to build the duties they owe to each other. Through this obligation there is justice. To illustrate his point he argues

The like natural inducement hath brought men to know that it is no less their duty to love others than themselves, for seeing those things which are equal, must needs all have one measure; if I cannot but wish to receive, even as much at every man's hands, as any man can wish unto his own soul, how should I look to have any part of my desire herein satisfied, unless myself be careful to satisfy the like desire, which is undoubtedly in other men weak, being one of the same nature.

This quote from Locke's ideas forever illustrates how he believes that justice is achieved by man's nature to be equal; Locke is saying that if people want something, then they have an obligation to produce something just as substantial as what they want. This reciprocity generates justice; this justice reflects the needs of man: if you do not want something, you should not produce anything that has the capabilities of being disliked. Based on Locke's idea of liberalism; if you wanted an apple, you would have to give something that equates the apple. This want makes people equal, because it is understood that if something is wanted, something of the same value has to be given. This mutual obligation produces not only equality but also justice; if the demands did not meet the needs of the mutual obligation, then an inequality would be present and consequently there would also be injustice.

Locke believed that man's nature would ultimately be the arbiter of justice. According to Locke, man's natural state is to be free; anyone who infringes man's natural freedom has now become susceptible of waging war. Locke describes this relationship of freedom and war stating "he who attempts to get another man into his absolute power does hereby put himself into a state of war with him." This natural state shows how the infringement of freedom compromises the human state of equality, and upsets the balance of justice.

John Stuart Mill was an influential mind during the eighteenth century. Mill believed in utilitarianism. Utilitarianism is the idea that the moral worth of an action is determined solely by its contribution to overall utility. Mill's idea of liberty shows conflict between the Liberty of will with society and civilization. Mill believes that the nature of society and limitations of civilization compromises the power exercised over an individual. Mill believes that the relationship between society and liberty of will have been undermined when looking at freedom stating "A question seldom stated, and hardly ever discussed, in general terms, but which profoundly influences the practical controversies of the age by its latent presence, and is likely soon to make itself recognized as the vital question of the future." This statement illustrates the role that society has played in the history of individual liberty. It also illustrates how these limitations that society has placed on individual liberty causes friction between the two factors and stresses change for the future. As this friction arises, it allows society to see what is wrong and change it for better conditions. Mill argues that this conflict has always existed and will continue to exist, duly because it is human nature.

We have witnessed the greatest minds have had their definition of liberalism. King and Locke have agreed that freedom, equality and justice are major components in liberalism. Mill's definition of the conflict of civil and social liberties and Locke's explanation on the state of war clarifies the actions taken by King in Birmingham; due to the dissatisfaction of blacks throughout the south, they boycotted long enough to have segregation ended in less than a year. They have all agreed that when either society or another person infringes upon liberties, that human nature will naturally fight, because it is an inherent value in mankind. Locke pointed out that mankind has the natural state of freedom, and anyone who infringes upon this freedom has waged war. When the clergymen sent that letter to King, they did not know that they and the south have long waged war against blacks by denying them liberty, but because blacks endured injustice for so long it allowed injustice to seem like justice. King's actions of civil disobedience not only reflected Locke's ideas of liberalism, but it also showed the paradigm of Mill's understanding between the liberty of will and the limitations that society holds on individual freedom. King's actions were justified, whites waged war on blacks first by denying liberty, and blacks are fighting back, because according to Locke it is human nature to be free. Anyone who is denied freedom is considered less than human, and that is just what "blacks" were viewed as; less than human. It took King to remind the south as well as America that "blacks" are indeed people and deserve freedom.

As we all see now, liberalism can be compared to fine wine; "It only gets better with age." This quote is an analogy to Mill's belief of liberty of how time is the ultimate determining factor of civil and social freedom. King, Locke, and Mill have all agreed that man has the right to their own well being, but most importantly they have all acknowledged society as well as other individuals as well as society play a major role of infringement in liberalism. As time continues to progress, we only get better. King fought for liberalism in the United States; forty-five years later we have a president that transcends race. Liberalism will forever be one of the many factors that contribute to the evolution of mankind. Unfortunately, due to the constant ignorance of illusion interruption it will always be seen as untimely and unwise, but it is freedom revelation that will always remind ignorance that liberty is never untimely and unwise.

"We don't own your laws; we don't own your country; we stand here as free, under God's sky, as you are; and, by the great God that made us, we'll fight for our liberty till we die."

So where does that leave us?

Revolution presents itself in many ways, and often has many faces; but the thing you can count on that all revolutionaries have is unity. Their blood boils with change; so much that you can see it in their eyes. Eyes are the light to the soul, so all revolutionaries should have the look same look you have. This means that martyrs should have the look of blissfulness, because their pictures are prefect. Revolutions always change and because they always change, they are never predicted. These sudden changes divide the drug-addict from the drug dealer, the drug- dealer from the "sell-out," **the niggers from the racists, the rebels from the revolutionary and ultimately; the martyr from the messiah.** "All that is bitter ends sweet and all that is sweet ends bitter" **this is revolution; revolutionaries are always rebels at one time and rebels are always revolutionaries at another. Knowing the capacity of revolution forces us to make the biggest decision of self- identity; Are we martyrs or are we messiahs?**

...I am Socrates **I am** Plato **I am** Gorgias **I am** Diocletian **I am** Constantine **I am** Malcolm X **I am** Martin Luther King Jr. **I am** Huey P. Newton **I am** Margaret Kuhn **I am** Cointelpro **I am** James Baldwin **I am** Susan B. Anthony **I am** Sojourner Truth **I AM** Uncle Tom **I am** Huckleberry Finn **I am** Willy Loman **I am** Pecola Breedlove **I am** Maureen Peal **I am** Holden Caulfield **I am** Atticus Finch **I am** Abraham Lincoln **I am** Mao Zedong **I am** Winston Churchill **I am** the Ku Klux Klan **I am** the Black Panthers **I am** Paul **I am** Galileo **I am** Leo Frank **I am** "sivilized" **I am** "phony" **I am** Maya Angelou **I am** Mary Wollstonecraft **I am** Oliver North **I am** Rich Porter **I am** N.W.A **I am** Tyler Durden **I am** 9/11 **I am** Heath

Legder **I am** 808s & Heartbreaks **I am** the nigger **and I am** the racist *I AM* REVOLUTION!!!

"You either die a hero or you live long enough to see yourself become the villain."

Every revolution needs a protagonist and an antagonist...

"I was a-trembling, because I'd got to decide, forever, betwixt two things, and I knowed it. I studied a minute, sort of holding my breath, and then says to myself, "All right, then, I'll" be your villain.

Don't take any of this dogmatically, because this is just another illusion interruption..."

"But one thing's for sure, nothing's for sure"

"Oh yeah, I almost forgot! Only racists get offended by niggers. You wanna stop sayin' nigga, stop being racist. But that would ruin everything… Wouldn't it?"

"You can tell a nigger wrote this."

"I bet a racist would say that."

"And for all you grammar coaches who feel I've made errors, I got a question for you."

"If I have a purpose for my mistakes are they still mistakes?"

"Can you still point a nigger out?"

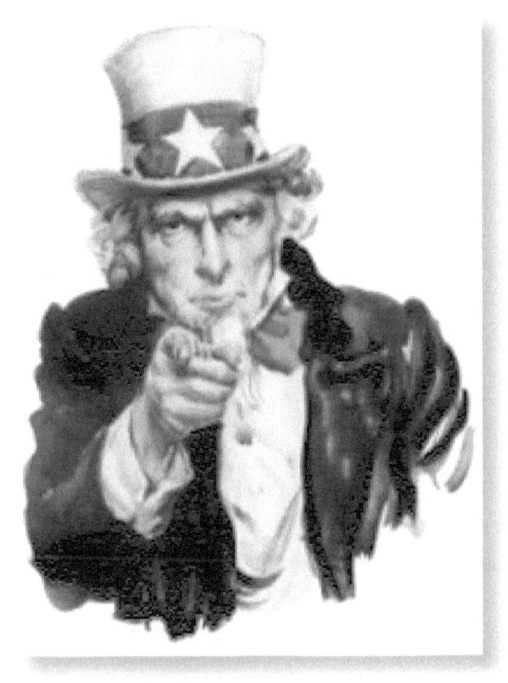

Still don't think you're a nigga? Well there's 10 ways to find out

If your mother and father had sex, then you're a nigga

If you have experienced the common cold, then you're a nigga

If you have ever owned a pencil, you're a nigga

If you didn't notice that the whole book is in quotation marks, you're a nigga

If you ever dialed the wrong number and then hung up, you're a nigga

If you've receive an award that spelled your name wrong, you're a nigga

If you believe in gravity, you're a nigga

If you've read this book, then you're a nigga

And If you've read this book and said "Why is the Finding Nemo chapter so long?" then skipped it, you're a nigga

If even one of these things apply to you then you're a nigga

Sorry Nigga, there's always racism

But no one wants to be racist?

Or do they?

"So how was that for a first book?"

"The funniest things are the forbidden."

"So was it good?"

"Honesty is the best policy - when there is money in it."

"Well I don't have any money yet."

"Goddam money. It always ends up making you blue as hell."

"Well that's you Holden, the things that make you blue ironically make you happy, I think. I guess Mark is being honest, I guess."

"If you really want to hear about it, the first thing you'll probably want to know is where I was born and what my lousy childhood was like, and how my parents were occupied and all before they had me, and all that David Copperfield kind of crap, but I don't feel like going into it, if you want to know the truth."

"Holden, what the fuck are you talking about?"

"People always think something's *all* true."

'You callin' me naïve nigga?"

"People never notice anything."

"I notice enough, I just want feedback on the book."

"It means nothing to me. I have no opinion about it, and I don't care."

"Damn, I wasn't expecting that Picasso, I thought what I was doing was real genius"

"Genius is personality with two pennies of talent."

"Well I have two pennies, but that's all I have."

"I like to live poor... but with a lot of money."

"LMAO, you got it nigga, so do you like the book? Can I get an answer from anyone?"

"Ask, and it will be given to you; seek, and you will find; knock, and it will be opened to you."

"That sounds familiar, oh my God! Aren't you?"

"I am who I am."

"... Oh shit! I mean um damn um excuse me but am I in trouble?"

"Why are ye fearful, O ye of little faith?"

"I have faith, that's why I wrote the book."

"Thou hast said."

"... I honestly have no response to that"

"What will ye that I shall do unto you?"

"I just want to know if the book is as good as you."

"Why callest thou me good? there is none good but one, that is, God: but if thou wilt enter into life, keep the commandments."

"Because that's what everyone calls you."

"Hear, and understand: Not that which goeth into the mouth defileth a man; but that which cometh out of the mouth, this defileth a man."

"I gotchu, I gotchu, I understand so I've been lied to about you?"

"A lie can make it half way around the world before the truth has time to put its boots on."

"I thought He wore sandals... and I thought you weren't talking unless I gave you money."

"A man is never more truthful than when he acknowledges himself a liar."

"Fair enough."

"You shall know the truth, and the truth shall set you free."

"When I found the truth out I started to tell other people but the more educated someone was the harder it was to free them I guess"

"I was born intelligent, education ruined me."

"There was a time when I used to get beat for misspelling education because I was first told to "Spell it how it sounds." So I spelled it e-d-u-k-s-h-u-n. Then I was told that's not how you spell it, and was told that it was spelled e-d-u-c-a-t-i-o-n. And I was always wondering how does *tion* makes *shun*?"

"They spell it "Vinci" and pronounce it "Vinchy". Foreigners always spell better than they pronounce."

"But isn't English the main language of America?"

"Whenever you find that you are on the side of the majority, it is time to reform."

"…LMAO, I get it, so about the money---"

"[The human race], in its poverty, has unquestionably one really effective weapon — laughter, Some men worship rank, some worship heroes, some worship power, some worship God, & over these ideals they dispute & cannot unite — but they all worship money."

"So you're saying fuck the money?"

"I am opposed to millionaires, but it would be dangerous to offer me the position."

"Me too, you know what someone said? That all that was left for me to do was go in the streets and preach naked."

"Clothes make the man. Naked people have little or no influence on society."

"Yo Mark you my nigga! Critics are gonna have a ball tearing this book apart!"

"The trade of critic, in literature, music, and the drama, is the most degraded of all trades."

"I never met anybody who said when they were a kid, 'I wanna grow up and be a critic.'"

"Richie! Twain what you think of the writing."

"If you had a million years to do it in, you couldn't rub out even half the 'Fuck you' signs in the world. It's impossible."

"I know Holden, the cursing was a bit much but sometimes filth is the only thing people acknowledge."

"Many a small thing has been made large by the right kind of advertising."

"I don't have a publicist yet and I bet they're all promising to steer clear of me."

"To promise not to do a thing is the surest way in the world to make a body want to go and do that very thing."

"I knew it, but it's one thing I learned from talking to all of you about my life."

"Always do right. This will gratify some people, and astonish the rest."

"Yea, but not that it's---"

"Be respectful to your superiors, if you have any."

"If you're not ready to die for it, take the word "freedom" out of your vocabulary."

"To stop a war, you must start one."

"True peace is not merely the absence of tension: it is the presence of justice."

"Beyond the walls of intelligence, life is defined"

"No evil can happen to a good man, neither in life nor after death."

"Man is the microcosm: I am my world."

"If you surrendered to the air, you could *ride* it."

"Any mind that is capable of a *real sorrow* is capable of good."

"Blessed are those who are persecuted because of righteousness, for theirs is the kingdom of heaven."

"Damn, can I say it.?"

"What happens to a dream deferred? "

"I'm never gonna change if ya'll don't allow to me to do it on my own. I gotta do this."

"Say it Loud!"

"I'm a nigger and I'm Proud!!! But it's one more thing I gotta break down."

"Let it be broke "

"A good person admits that they're not the greatest person, see ya'll in Sweden."

"What's There?"

"You'll see, and I never got a damn answer for my book… Smh. Niggas."

OUTRÉ

Talent is hindsight, genius is foresight, and intellect is blind. Our Blind Ambition has anomalous vision. Our vision is not twenty-twenty, for we cannot see what's going on now. Instead, we see things that have yet to exist. We are naïve to present situations, but aware of future ones. Eyes are one sided windows that are incapable of looking inward. We cannot see what Blind Ambition does to us, to our vision, it doesn't exist. Just because we can't see it, doesn't mean it's not there. We often run into the same problems because we are unable to avoid oncoming predicaments. Illegally, we live legally blind lives. Because we are perceived to not see, we see everything but, the world could never know. This is our big secret. If everyone knew that Blind Ambition shapes the imminent and inevitable, our eyes would be carved into ironic liars. We know what's going on but we refuse to acknowledge its truth. If we see nothing, then nothing can change. However, if we are suspected of having the same windows as everyone else, they would shatter under the constant pressure of opening our shutters. We hide behind our blinds because it prevents us from doing anything. As long as we keep the shutters closed, we can open doors that will allow our Blind Ambition to wander freely. Free vision is an outward reflection as oppose to an inward one. Because we cannot see our own Blind Ambition, we have to look at everyone else's. Eyes are the light to the soul, but moreover, they are mirrors. Without mirrors, no one knows they exist. We depend on our eyesight to mirror a reflection that agrees with our perfection, but because our mirrors usually fail in accomplishing this task, we rely on everyone else. Unfortunately, no one can see their own mirror without looking at someone else's. Blind Ambition is distorted by intelligence. Tragedy is the real triumph. Weakness, however, is beneath us therefore we can't see it. We stay on Ground Zero because we're blind to our altitude. Every time our weakness is shown, our Blind Ambition rebuilds our Achilles Heel.

We stand strong by Blind Ambition; it blinds us of hell without telling us we're seeing heaven. Our Life is going to be the Death of us. The things we love, hate us. Passion becomes our crush. Ambition is the unrequited love that passes us by and never acknowledges us as an entity. Because Ambition refuses to recognize us, we will present ourselves in a new light. Our divine right of being noticed proves potent. Even though Ambition hangs in the Halls of Greatness, we are not allowed there yet. Without Accomplishment, there is no Recognition. Without Recognition there is no Existence. When Opportunity presents itself, we will take Passion and make Ambition jealous. This unrequited love will become mutual. And when Ambition loves us as much as we love Passion, we will leave both for Greatness. Greatness will acknowledge Existence through Accomplishment and our illusion will become everlasting. Then we, too, can echo in the Halls of Greatness. WE ARE HISTORY. We replace our empathies with sympathies. When we look at things, we don't feel with, we feel for. But how could you? You've never lived in my Age of Greatness, so my importance is irrelevant to you. Our fear of living comes with our fear of losing. For everyday we are remembered, we are forgotten. Although we're omnipotent, our ambivalence causes people to tire of us easily. We're not talked about as much. People will about us, but rarely will people understand and appreciate our contributions to the present. If you want to cheat Death you have to be honest with Life. we have lied to both, so where does that leave us? But I ask of you one thing, please don't forget me. Obligation is an obligation to the fool. This reflects the one who takes it and the one who makes it. A promise is nothing more than a novelty that serves a purpose for the time being. Yes we all love new things, but preserving freshness spoils us. Nothing can ever be preserved, and our attempts to disprove this remains to be seen. We are indeed intelligent. One step above talent and one below genius, this is us. We are the middle generation that uses the talent of the predecessor and the genius of the imminent to define ourselves. We are alert and quick-witted. We are never predicted, but we are always accounted for. And yet, even in our quick-wit, we are easily defeated by the long anticipated novel promises we try to uphold. We deplore talent and canonize genius with our intellect but never understand either. So we reduce our freshness and call it novel, we reuse our new and call it vintage, we recycle our vintage and call it fresh. And all the while we are present. The present is the promise that can never be kept. And because we always try to preserve its freshness, we are always spoiled by the future. We can never be forgotten, because we are always here. Heaven is not a promise, it's an incentive. Pray for me. I'm not affected by affection. Some people cry over spilled milk, some people watch their milk spill, but there is no sense in crying over something you'll never have; this is me. I will come in due time, but not when you want me to. You will never see me coming no matter how hard you try. Out of nothing come me, chaos is my nickname. Alpha and Omega are my friends, for we have done much work together. The future is not complicated; people just tend to complicate it. There is no past or present in my presence because I've plagiarized both. Speculation does not foreshadow my arrival nor does it do me any justice. Instead, it only misleads and slanders my name. When you look at me wear shades, otherwise I'll destroy your perspective. You don't have to remember me because I'll never forget you. It's hard being around when no one can see you. I don't exist. Trying to prove I do will be the death of you. We are Timeless. We make our heavens and our hells, we make our gods and our devils, we make our saviors and our menaces, we destroy ourselves and we build ourselves up, our salvations define our damnations. This blasphemy is what makes us human. Greatness is defined by motivation without obligation. It's easier for us to do things when it is expected, but what happens when we aren't expected to do anything? This is what defines miracles, phenomenon, and legends. Many great people have done exceptional tasks due to obligation, but the ones who stand out are those who do the same things without conscience. Their clear conscious is not concerned with debts to society, because they owe society nothing. Society makes the individual, the individual makes society and that's it. There are no remainders in life; everyone is square from the moment they enter to the moment they exit. Art is made to critique nature; nature is here to critique art. Having a dream is like throwing a ball in the air. We throw it as far as we can, then wait to see how long it takes to come down. If it takes too long, we forget it. If it comes down quicker than expected we become bored. Reality is the no man's land for our dreams. Although it seems like the safest place due to its vacancy, people tend to avoid the middle because of fear and uncertainty. No one plays the middle for fear of immediate death from both sides of opposition. People become so fearful that they seek security and protection. This security entails becoming educated, informed and led. The leaders are just as fearful as the followers, so everyone becomes entrapped within timidness. But you know who changes it? The nigga who waits for that ball to come down. Patience evokes fear, fear evokes change, and change evokes revolution. Revolution is life.

In 2012, the world won't end, it'll be highly outré.